GOOD HOUSEKEEPING
50 Beautiful things to make

Edited by Shirley Green

EBURY
PRESS

Published by Ebury Press
National Magazine House
72 Broadwick Street
London W1V 2BP

First Impression 1982

ISBN 0 85223 245 4 (hardback)
ISBN 0 85223 256 X (paperback)

Consultant Diana Austen
Design by Tim Foster
Artist John Woodcock

Filmset in Great Britain by
Advanced Filmsetters (Glasgow) Ltd

Printed and bound in Yugoslavia by
Mladinska knjiga, Ljubljana

GOOD HOUSEKEEPING
50 Beautiful things to make

Contents

Introduction

This book is for all creative people who love making beautiful things with their hands. Truly beautiful things that do not date, and will become the family heirlooms of tomorrow.

Some of them have already stood the test of time. They have appeared in Good Housekeeping over the years, and have proved so timeless in appeal that readers continually write to request back copies. Some of them are new in so far as they're newly commissioned—but there's nothing merely fashionable about them. When you're going to expend so much love and effort, we feel you deserve what's designed to last—this year, next year and forever.

In fact, most of the desirable items on the following pages demand more love than time or effort. They're surprisingly simple and quick to make. Others could take a week or even longer, and in the exceptional cases that might keep you busy for months,

we've tried to suggest acceptable short cuts to make time pass quickly.

What's more, none of them demands any difficult skills. They may look immensely accomplished when finished, but that's thanks to the skill of the original designs, which cleverly exploit everyday techniques and materials—using them to such unusual advantage that even beginners can get "expert" results.

Although the majority of the beautiful things in this book will surely be treasured by future generations, a few will vanish in a trice. For we've included a really wide variety from sea shell pictures and satin-bound towels to marzipan dates and chestnut crackles. But whatever their lifespan they share one thing in common. They're better—and cheaper—than anything in the shops. Each one is very, very special, and we hope you enjoy making them as much as we enjoyed finding them for you to make.

1

A touch of luxury

Whether you trim existing pillowcases or make your own from sheeting, the low-cost results in terms of time and money will prove super-rich and very ritzy.

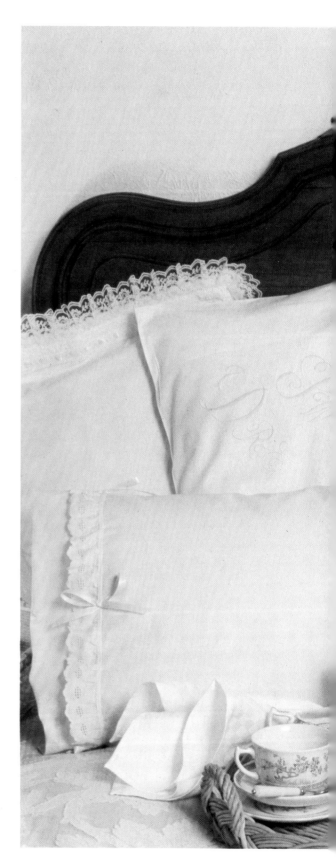

Provided you use plain pillowcases or sheeting, and keep to gentle, delicate shades like ivory, pale yellow, subtle pink, and white, the trimmings you add will look coolly chic rather than merely pretty-pretty. And if you use the materials we suggest, despite their fragile and elegant appearance, they'll also be practical and machine-washable. We give clockwise instructions for the pillowcases, starting with the top row at the left.

Two-tiered frilled pillowcase

Materials

9 m of 6.5 cm ($2\frac{1}{2}$ in) wide edging lace.
3 m of lace trimming ready-threaded with ribbon.
A corded pillowcase (All from John Lewis or John Lewis Partnership stores).

Method

Stitch the first layer of lace, ungathered, along the line of the cording, pleating around the corners. Place the second layer immediately behind and machine-stitch, pleating about every 3 cm ($1\frac{1}{4}$ in) as you go. To prevent the lace flopping forward, machine another line of stitching about 4 cm ($1\frac{1}{2}$ in) up from the cording line, through both layers of lace.

Stitch the lace with ready-threaded ribbon over the cording line to trim the inner edge neatly and appealingly.

Embroidered pillowcase

Materials

Single letter transfers (direct or mail order from The Danish House).
Anchor stranded cotton in 0293.
A pillowcase.

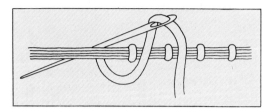

Method

Carefully space out the transfers and iron them onto the front of the pillowcase. Embroider the letters in satin stitch (see the diagram on page 85), and work all the narrow strokes of the letters, particularly where they are curved, in couching stitch as shown in the diagram on this page. To couch the narrow strokes, bring a length of stranded cotton through to the right side of the pillowcase and lay it along the line of the stroke. Bring another length of stranded cotton (this is known as the couching thread) through at the same place. Then, guiding the laid thread loosely with your left hand, with your right hand stitch it firmly into place at regular intervals in overcast stitch, using the couching thread, and always taking care that the laid thread is lying neatly underneath the overcast stitches.

Place the overcast stitches close together around an exaggerated curve, so that the laid thread lies flat; and if you have to couch a severe angle, make sure to place an overcast stitch at the point of the angle. When you have finished couching, return the laid thread to the wrong side of the pillowcase and secure. To achieve a really fine line of couching, you can, of course, use only one or two strands of the embroidery cotton, both for the laid and for the couching threads.

Ruched ribbon pillowcase

Materials

0.6 m of 1.25 cm ($\frac{1}{2}$ in) wide Offray's double-faced polyester satin ribbon.
0.7 m of 2 cm ($\frac{3}{4}$ in) wide matching ribbon.
0.8 m of 2.5 cm (1 in) wide matching ribbon (direct or mail order from Ries Wools of Holborn).
A pillowcase.

Method

Measure a line from top to bottom of the pillowcase 3 cm ($1\frac{1}{4}$ in) from the open end, and mark lightly with a pencil. Using the widest ribbon, make a long running stitch down its centre and gather until you have 6 cm ($2\frac{1}{2}$ in) of gathering. Make a small holding stitch to prevent the gathers from ungathering. Pin the ribbon to the pencil line as shown in the photograph and stitch, turning in the ribbon at the bottom edge of the pillowcase. Keeping all the ribbons 3 cm ($1\frac{1}{4}$ in) apart, repeat with the two other ribbons, but gather a 12 cm ($4\frac{3}{4}$ in) length for the medium width ribbon, and an 18 cm (7 in) length for the narrowest ribbon.

Scallop-edged pillowcase

Materials

1 m of 230 cm (90 in) wide white sheeting—this is enough to make two pillowcases.
0.2 m of 90 cm (36 in) wide polyester wadding to pad the edges.
Ivory thread (All from John Lewis and John Lewis Partnership stores).

Method

Cut a piece of sheeting 60 cm ($23\frac{1}{2}$ in) by 80 cm ($31\frac{1}{2}$ in) for the back of the pillowcase, and a piece 60 cm ($23\frac{1}{2}$ in) by 100 cm ($39\frac{1}{2}$ in) for the front. This allows 20 cm (8 in) for the pillow flap. Cut a paper pattern for the scallops, making it five scallops wide. Overall, it should measure 15 cm (6 in) wide by a maximum of 3 cm ($1\frac{1}{4}$ in) high. With a pencil, use the pattern to draw the scallop shapes along the edges of the back of the pillowcase. As the pillow flap forms the fourth edge, draw scallop shapes along its back too. You will find you can fit the pattern three times along each short side and four times along each long side. It's best to set it in from the edges to make sewing easier.

Hem one short edge of the pillow-case back. Work first along the edge with the pillow flap. Inset a 6 cm ($2\frac{3}{8}$ in) strip of wadding and straight-stitch around the pencilled scallop line and about 4.5 cm ($1\frac{3}{4}$ in) down the interior shell lines for that edge only. Then pin the front and back of the pillowcase together, right sides out and with the strips of wadding between. Continue the stitching sequences as above, through all thicknesses. With close zigzag or buttonhole stitch, machine round the scalloped edges. Cut away the excess fabric close to the line of stitching, and zigzag over the edge again for a neat, non-fray finish.

Pillowcase with corner trimmings

Materials

1 m of fine, soft edging lace, about 20 cm (8 in) wide.
2 m of narrow satin ribbon.
A pillowcase or sheeting (All from John Lewis and John Lewis Partnership stores).

Method

Unpick an existing pillowcase or cut a pillowcase front, 50 cm ($19\frac{1}{2}$ in) by 90 cm (36 in) and back, 50 cm ($19\frac{1}{2}$ in) by 70 cm ($27\frac{1}{2}$ in) as described. Cut the lace into four equal lengths and place diagonally over the four corners of the pillowcase front. Pin and stitch into position. Set two short lengths of ribbon diagonally across the lace as shown in the photograph, and stitch into position. Trim the excess lace to

leave a seam allowance equal to the seam allowance of the pillowcase.

With right sides together, stitch (or re-stitch) the pillowcase together so the seams incorporate the lace. Turn the pillowcase right sides out.

Frilled pillowcase with appliqued ribbon

Materials

2.6 m of 5 cm (2 in) wide pre-frilled eyelet edging in ivory (from John Lewis and John Lewis Partnership stores).
2.5 m of 4 cm ($1\frac{1}{2}$ in) wide Offray's double-faced polyester satin ribbon in ivory (direct or mail order from Ries Wools of Holborn).
A pillowcase.

Method

Trim the pillowcase with the frill, stitching it into the seam by making a run-and-fell or French seam at the join. Arrange the ribbon freely as shown in the photograph, allowing long ends and making the bow near a top corner where it will not cause discomfort. Pin the ribbon into place, and hand sew neatly and securely.

Frilled and bow-trimmed pillow-case

Materials

0.5 m of 5 cm (2 in) wide pre-frilled eyelet edging in ivory (from John Lewis as previously).
1.5 m of 1 cm ($\frac{3}{8}$ in) wide Offray's double-faced polyester satin ribbon in ivory (from Ries Wools as previously).
A pillowcase.

Method

Stitch the frill 6 cm ($2\frac{3}{8}$ in) from the open edge of the pillowcase. Make three identical satin bows and stitch at the top, the bottom, and in the centre of the frill, attaching them at their centres only, so the loops and tails are free.

2

An enchantingly pretty perfumed pomander

Pomanders were once believed to ward off illness. In fact, they only ward off moths—but that's as good a reason as any to hang one in the wardrobe.

Originally, pomanders were small amber-like balls of blended aromatic substances. The French called them amber-apples or "pomme d'ambre"—which is how our word pomander came about. They were kept in perforated containers called pouncet boxes, which could be attached to a belt or worn round the neck. But sometimes they were rolled into smaller, bead-like balls, and threaded to make conventional necklaces and bracelets. Even when people no longer believed that pomanders gave protection against the plague, they still wore them to scent their bodies and their clothes. Properly made, they retained their smell for years.

A few enthusiasts still make them in the traditional way, laboriously pulverising obscure ingredients and melting them into a treacly mess that solidifies into a rock hard substance. (See page 122 if you'd like to join them). But we've preferred a much simpler pomander that will still retain its fragrance for many months and impart it gradually to its surroundings.

Materials

A fresh, firm but thin-skinned orange.
Ground cinnamon.
Mace.
Powdered orris root.
Large-headed Penang cloves (All spices direct or mail order from Meadow Herbs).
A knitting needle.
A cocktail stick.
Some ends of ribbon.
A few dried flower heads.
A miniature wicker basket (direct or mail order from a selection at The Neal Street Shop).

Method

Mix the ground cinnamon, mace and powdered orris root together in a bowl. If you haven't come across orris root before, it derives from the Florentine iris, and not only yields its own sweet violet-like scent but acts as a fixative for other perfumes.

Take the orange, and pierce it across the middle sideways with the knitting needle. Pack as much of the spice mixture as possible into the hole. Then, with the cocktail stick, punch holes deeply all over the orange, ideally working in lines from top to bottom. Sprinkle a little of the spice mixture into all the holes, and stick in the cloves, aiming for a close fit so they won't fall out as the orange shrinks. You may, however, find it easier to work in sections, punching just a small block of holes at a time, and sprinkling in the spices and sticking in the cloves as you go.

Once the pomander is bristling all over with cloves, place it in the bowl of mixed powdered spices, and leave it for several days, rotating daily so that every part of the surface is permeated.

Later, if you want to hang the pomander in the wardrobe, simply tie a ribbon round it with a loop at the top, making sure to position the ribbon so it covers the knitting needle holes.

But if you want to put the pomander on something like a dressing table, where it will be in full view, it's worth decorating it as shown in the photograph. Place some narrow satin ribbon on a wider lacy ribbon (if it misbehaves, stick it in position with a light dab of Copydex), and tie it into an elaborate bow at the top. Then pin the dried flower heads around the middle of the orange—pinning quite literally with long dress-making pins. Finally, sit the pomander in the miniature wicker basket; or sit it in a saucer filled with more dried flower heads.

3

Lighting up time

You can make swirly candles, layered candles, frosted candles, embossed candles. You can even make pressed-flower-decorated candles. But plain, traditionally dipped candles are probably still the most beautiful.

Because making candles is as easy as toffee (very similar too in many respects), people often feel obliged to try complicated effects. They also strive for a look of such glossy perfection, that the results are indistinguishable from mass-produced shop products. Obviously homemade candles need to work efficiently, and we're not suggesting they should look lumpish or misshapen, but they should have an individuality that makes them better than anything mere money can buy.

Our traditionally dipped candles are a case in point. Although we could have used a special overdipping wax, which would have given them a hard and shiny surface, we preferred to stick to the ordinary wax, which leaves a soft, and attractively matt finish. And although we could have used much denser colour and kept it uniform throughout the entire batch of candles, we preferred the merest whispers of pink, which we varied slightly with each pair. Finally, although we could have mixed the dyes with a special whitener to achieve a more solid and opaque pink, we preferred to use the dyes in minute quantities, which achieves a pale and translucent finish.

Old-fashioned dipped candles

Materials

To make three pairs of candles, about 23 cm (9 in) long by 1.25 cm ($\frac{1}{2}$ in) to 2 cm ($\frac{3}{4}$ in) wide, you'll need:
3 kg (7 lb) of paraffin wax—the quantity needed for dipping, though there will be lots left over.
Three 1.25 cm ($\frac{1}{2}$ in) wicks, 55 cm ($21\frac{1}{2}$ in) long. Each wick makes a pair of candles simultaneously.
A dipping can at least 2.5 cm (1 in) taller than the 23 cm (9 in) long candles.
Wax-soluble dye discs in cerise pink, brick red and yellow. (All direct or mail order from Candle Maker Supplies.)
A cooking thermometer.

Method

Melt the wax in the dipping can, and maintain the molten wax at a constant temperature of about 71°C (160°F). Be very careful not to overheat the wax, because like cooking oil it's potentially dangerous, and could catch fire if it rises above 149°C (300°F).

Priming the wicks: Fold one of the wicks in half, and pick it up at its centre, so it hangs down about 27 cm ($10\frac{1}{2}$ in) either side. This, in effect, creates two wicks. Dip them in the molten wax for about one minute, keeping your fingers well clear of the wax. Remove the wicks, and as they cool, pull them straight, and hang up for at least a minute. Repeat the process with the other two 55 cm ($21\frac{1}{2}$ in) lengths of wick.

Dipping the candles: Pick up one

of the primed wicks by its unprimed centre, and dip it back in the molten wax for about three seconds. Remove it, and hang up to cool for at least one minute. Keep on dipping and hanging in this way, and you will see a pair of candles grow before your eyes as the wax builds up gradually coat by coat— but make sure the candles don't touch during the "tacky" stage of cooling. Leave the two candles joined by their common wick for the time being. Repeat the dipping and hanging process for the other two pairs of candles, building up to the required thickness.

Dyeing the candles: The dye discs come in strong, bright colours, and although it's possible to intermix them, if you overdo it, they tend to look sludgy. As we only wanted the palest of shades, we mixed tiny quantities of the cerise pink and brick red, and added just the smallest touch of yellow. Even so, it was largely a matter of trial and error. We varied the shade for each pair of candles, strengthening the colour as we went.

Floating on water: Each dye disc will colour about 500 gms ($17\frac{1}{2}$ oz) of wax, so you could make up a lot of coloured wax, fill the cleaned-out dipping can nearly full, and dip the candles exactly as before. But it's much more economical to make up just a little coloured wax, part-fill the dipping can with hot water, and float the coloured wax on the surface. Then you can dip the candles through it into the water, pulling the candles out quickly again.

To use the economical method, partly fill the dipping can with water and heat it to 88°C (190°F). Gently pour in 50 ml (2 oz) of coloured wax and maintain the temperature at 82°C (180°F). Then dip the candles, once, twice, or even three times, depending on the strength of colour you'd like.

When dipping is completed, cut the wicks to separate the pairs of candles, trim off the candle bases with a knife, and leave to cool for about an hour.

To make the cylindrical candles here and on the cover

Once you start making moulded candles, you need to add 10% of a substance called stearin to the paraffin wax, so that the candles shrink and leave their moulds cleanly. As stearin also raises the melting point of the wax, the result is a longer-burning and more opaque candle. In addition, of course, you need a mould.

Materials

To make two 7.5 cm (3 in) high by 5 cm (2 in) wide candles, you'll need:
225 grms (8 oz) of paraffin wax.
25 grms (1 oz) of stearin.
A 5 cm (2 in) wick, 20 cm (8 in) long.
One eighth of a dye disc (for subtle shading, mixing colours from different dye discs to make up the amount).
A wick rod—anything at least 2.5 cm (1 in) wider than the cylindrical mould that will sit lightly across its surface—say a skewer or a pencil.
A cylindrical metal mould.
A thermometer to check temperature.
Some mould seal, which is rather like putty. (All available from Candle Maker Supplies.)

Method

Melt the stearin over a low heat in an old saucepan, and add the fraction of dye disc. When all the dye has dissolved, add the paraffin wax, bringing it to a temperature of 82°C (180°F) and maintaining it there. Lower the wick into the wax to prime it, straighten as it cools, and leave it to cool completely.

Threading the wick: You will find the mould has a hole at its base. Thread the primed wick up through the hole, leaving a generous "tail" at the bottom, and tie the top of the wick to the wick rod. Making sure the wick rod is resting across the full diameter of the top of the mould, pull the "tail" so the wick tightens, and secure the "tail" taut with a lump of mould seal. Check that the hole in the base is leakproof.

Filling the mould: Pour the wax, still at 82°C (180°F), carefully into the mould. Wait for about a minute, and give the mould a sharp tap to release any air trapped on the surface. Now stand the mould in a bowl of cold water, and hold it down with a weight.

Topping up operations: After an hour, you will find a well has formed in the wax around the wick. If this is allowed to set, a cavity will form in the candle's centre, causing the outer walls to distort. Fortunately, it's easy to avoid disaster. Remove the mould from the water, and pierce the area around the wick with a needle. Then heat the leftover wax in the saucepan to 93°C (200°F), and top up the candle, making sure not to fill above the original level. If you do, the wax will seep down between the candle and the mould, making it difficult to remove and spoiling its finish. Replace the mould in cold water for a further hour, until the candle has thoroughly set.

Turning out the candle: Remove the mould seal from the base of the mould, and the candle will slip out instantly. What was the bottom will, of course, now be the top. Neaten the base of the candle by trimming the wick back, and levelling the wax by rubbing it gently over the bottom of an empty, heated saucepan.

Improvising moulds: Once you start making moulded candles, you'll probably be tempted to improvise all sorts of moulds. It won't be difficult finding suitable subjects. Almost any smooth-surfaced container will do, provided they can withstand the heat of molten wax, and are capable of having a hole made through their base. Old milk cartons, yoghurt cups, fruit juice canisters—or even egg shells can be brought into candle-making service. And so can biscuit cutters—as you'll see if you look at our heart and star-shaped candles.

Putting biscuit cutters to use: We made our tiny tart-shaped candles by standing a set of biscuit cutters on a smooth, shiny surface, and anchoring them there with plenty of mould seal, which also made them completely leak-proof. Then we poured in the wax (made exactly as for the cylindrical candle), and left it till nearly set.

Using a wicking needle: At this stage, we threaded a primed wick through a special wicking needle (also available from Candle Maker Supplies), and threaded each candle with a short length of wick. Then we lifted our moulds, complete with mould seal, and cooled the whole lot in a shallow pan of cold water.

Although we melted fresh wax for these candles, they're so small they'd make an ideal way of using up leftovers from bigger candles.

Candles in action: Delicate-coloured candles look beautiful unlit, but they're rather ordinary when actually burning. This is especially true if the basic candle is white, with only one or two coats of colour on the surface. However, candles made from strong-coloured wax throughout, though they may look a bit garish in the cold light of day, come into their own when they're finally lit. They glow with a wonderful rich, intense light.

A practical footnote: It's important to match the size of wick to the size of your candle, because candles burn like old-fashioned oil lamps. The fuel gets drawn up the wick by capillary action.

If a wick is too thick for the diameter of a candle, there won't be enough fuel to keep it fed, and it will start burning itself up, causing soot and smoke. But if the wick is too small it will splutter and die, drowned in a pool of molten wax.

Most wicks are sold in 1.25 cm ($\frac{1}{2}$ in) gradations, which doesn't mean the wicks themselves are that thick—but that they're intended for candles with those diameters. Regardless of size, they should always be trimmed to 1.25 cm ($\frac{1}{2}$ in) before lighting.

4

A fabulous paper-patchwork screen

**Anyone who's toiled for years
on a conventional patchwork will appreciate
the simplicity of this screen.
Despite its wealth of visual complexity
—there's not a single stitch in sight.**

Most short-cuts give inferior results. But this rich and satisfying paper-patchwork looks as good as anything made from fabric at the cost of pricked fingers and endless eye-strain. Colours keep to basic shades of brown, which gives it a warm and mellow look. But if you don't want browns, you could easily choose another colour, and confine yourself to its various shades. Or, if you're confident about mixing colours, and feel you could get the "balance" right, you could run the whole gamut of the spectrum. The black background will hold good for any strong, deep tones, but if you prefer much lighter shades, you could paint the screen in a lighter colour.

Materials

An old screen—either wooden or covered in a tight-woven canvas that can be overpainted. (If you don't already have a screen, try local junk or second-hand shops. Or try making one. All it takes is three wooden frames that you can cover with canvas and hinge together. *NB* The tight-woven canvas you need is medium-weight cotton duck canvas. If you can't find it locally, it's available direct and mail order from Russell & Chapple. Or you could use much cheaper unbleached calico, provided you paint it with a coat of size first.)
Black emulsion or gloss paint.

Bits of wallpaper (best way to get a good variety is to beg the old pattern books from a decorating shop).
The colour pages from all those glossy magazines you've been hoarding.
NB Although this screen was papered entirely from wallpaper and magazine colour-pages, you could, of course, use wrapping paper, glossy gardening catalogues—or anything pretty that appeals to you.
A 1.25 cm ($\frac{1}{2}$ in) hexagon "window" template. (Available from local craft shops; or direct and mail order from The Patchwork Dog).
A pair of *sharp* scissors—accuracy of cutting is essential.
A tube of Copydex glue—for use on a canvas-covered screen.
A tube of Uhu glue—for use on a wooden screen.
Winsor & Newton's paper varnish (from most art-shops).

Method

Paint the entire screen black. Cut out paper hexagons in sets of six—if you do too many in advance, they'll only get dog-eared. Because the template is made of clear plastic, you'll be able to see exactly what you're cutting out, and be sure of getting well-balanced areas of pattern. Do not draw round the template and then cut out, as this leads to fractional inaccuracies that eventually add up to major positioning problems. Instead, cut directly from

the template, holding it firmly to the paper as you go along.

To arrange the hexagons: start with the top row. Position each set of six patches into a flower shape, but leave the middle of the flower bare, so the black of the actual screen forms the centre hexagon. Take great care to get this row perfectly straight, with all horizontal lines at right angles to the vertical sides of the screen. Stick each patch firmly in position with the appropriate glue, making sure that each patch fits snugly against it's neighbour. When the first row of flowers is completed, work the next, following the positioning in the photograph, so that the bare areas of screen show through as small black triangle and diamond shapes.

When all the screen is covered, protect the patchwork flowers by applying a light coat of paper varnish. If you use an ordinary clear varnish, petals made from coloured pages of glossy magazines could become semi-transparent, and allow print on the obverse side to show through permanently.

5

A loom with a view

You don't have to know a warp from a weft to create our idyllically tranquil landscape. So even the rankest of beginners can weave a consummate work of art.

Most people think weaving is rather an advanced skill, demanding hard-learnt techniques and expensive equipment. But simple looms were invented over 6000 years ago, and even primitive tribes managed to devise some way of keeping vertical threads fixed and taut so that horizontal threads could be woven through them. Looms became more sophisticated throughout Europe, but very little changed essentially until the advent of the Industrial Revolution. Then mechanised weaving took over almost completely, with only small pockets of rural communities keeping alive the old art.

The loom that's needed for our pastoral tapestry is not one that derives from European tradition. It's much simpler and goes back to weaving's primitive beginnings. In fact, it's almost identical to the looms that are used by Navajo Indians in North America today. It has two advantages over anything else. You can make it yourself from cheap, basic ingredients with the absolute minimum of practical talent. And because it's very small and light, you can carry it around with you, weaving a few rows when the opportunity arises. Be prepared for it to attract more attention than knitting if you bring it out on the bus or a train.

Despite the adult appeal of its design, our tapestry is easy enough for a child to tackle. What's more, as the wooden loom is so good-looking, you can leave it in situ once the tapestry is completed to provide a perfect and permanent frame.

Materials

An artist's stretcher frame, 25 cm (9¾ in) by 30 cm (11¼ in) to act as the improvised loom (available from art shops).
Fine, non-elastic string to use for the warp (from craft shops).
A packet of 1.25 cm (½ in) tacks.
Some thick white card.
Coats Tapisserie wools: two skeins of 0246 and one each of 0218, 0269, 0268 and 0216, for the grass.
Anchor stranded cottons: one skein of 0245 and one of 0262, for the grass; two skeins of 0161 and one each of 0158 and 0160 for the sky; one skein of 0386 for the face and legs of the sheep.
White bouclé knitting wool for the sheep.
A kitchen fork.
A knitting needle.

Method

To set up the loom: Using the photograph as reference, pencil-mark on the stretcher frame the positions of the tacks as follows. Draw a vertical line down the centre of the top and bottom struts. Measure 6.5 cm (2½ in) either side of this line, and draw two more lines. Between these two outer lines,

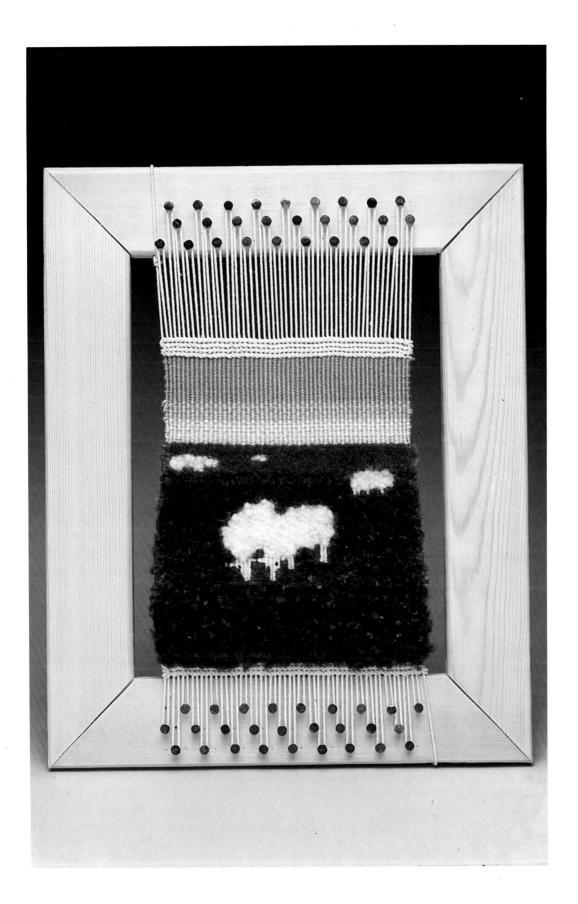

draw more vertical lines at 5 mm ($\frac{3}{16}$ in) intervals.

On the bottom strut, measure 1 cm ($\frac{3}{8}$ in), 2 cm ($\frac{3}{4}$ in) and 3 cm ($1\frac{1}{8}$ in) down from the inside edge of the frame, and draw three horizontal lines. On the top strut, measure 5 mm ($\frac{3}{16}$ in), 1.5 cm ($\frac{5}{8}$ in) and 2.5 cm (1 in) up from the inside edge, and draw three horizontal lines. Where the horizontal lines cross over the vertical lines, hammer in the tacks firmly.

Making the warp: To form the warp —ie the long downward threads—tie your string around the top strut, near the left-hand corner, as shown in the photograph. Lace the strings tautly up and down around the tacks. Finish by tying the string around the bottom strut, near the right-hand corner.

Now cut two strips of card, 1.5 cm ($\frac{5}{8}$ in) by 16 cm ($6\frac{1}{4}$ in). Thread one strip right through the warp from side to side, working over and under alternate threads, and push it down against the bottom tacks. (You will need this to give a firm, even edge to your first row of knots—otherwise they might travel down towards the tacks). Thread the other strip through the warp in the same way, but push it up against the top tacks. (You will need this strip to facilitate the actual weaving, because when it's stood on edge, it raises every alternate warp thread.)

Although the photograph on the previous page is considerably smaller than the real size of the tapestry, and should only be referred to for general guidance, the line-drawing of the sheep on the opposite page is shown actual size. This means it can be used as a precise design-guide as follows: cut a piece of card to the same dimensions as the stretcher frame, and trace onto it the line-drawing of the sheep. Then tape the card onto the back of the frame, and the drawing will show clearly through the warp to ensure that you get the scale and balance of the landscape's composition right.

To begin weaving: Take a length of string about 100 cm (40 in) long and wind it into a small ball. Starting at the bottom right, leave at least 8 cm (3 in) of string at the back, and work four rows of knots as shown in Diagram 1, catching the 8 cm (3 in) length into the back of the first knots as you go. (As you can see from the diagram, these knots are not knots in the conventional tied sense.) When you have completed these four rows, beat them down firmly with the prongs of the fork, so they're packed together as tightly as possible. Beat down subsequent rows of weaving in exactly the same way.

Tips for realistic effects: To give the landscape a sense of perspective, use darker colours in the foreground near the bottom of the frame, and lighter colours for the distant grass near the sky-line. To increase the realism still further, twine different shades of green together, sometimes mixing wool and stranded cotton.

The grass consists of one row of looped weaving, followed by two rows of plain weaving, followed by one row of looped weaving etc. To create the textured effect of rough-cropped pasture, work the looped rows in extra-thick wool, or wool and stranded cotton; but work the plain rows in single thickness only.

Each time a new colour is started, leave at least 8 cm (3 in) of wool or stranded cotton at the back, and either work it into the back of the first stitches as you go, or wait until the weaving is complete, and then darn all the ends in tidily.

To work the grass: Starting at the bottom right, and with a knitting needle placed across the warp, work a row of loops over the needle as shown in Diagram 2. (You need the knitting needle to make sure all your loops are the same size.) Next, work two rows of plain—a straightforward over-and-under stitch as shown beneath

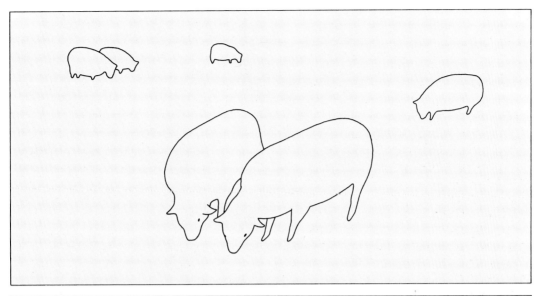

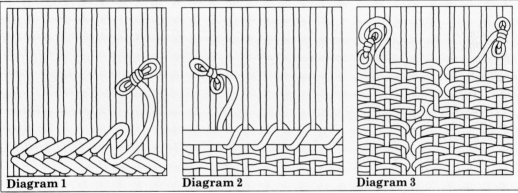

Diagram 1   **Diagram 2**   **Diagram 3**

the loops in Diagram 2. Then work another row of loops—and keep on working them until you have finally reached the sky-line.

To weave the sheep and sky: Work the sheep separately in plain weaving, as shown in Diagram 3. Use 0386 stranded cotton for the head and legs and white bouclé knitting wool for the body. Sew the eyes with black cotton.

Again using plain weaving, work the sky in 0158, 0160 and 0161 stranded cottons, referring to the photograph for your colour-guide. As with the grass, occasionally twine different shades together—but keep the thickness of the strands constant.

When you have reached the top of the sky, cut another 100 cm (40 in) length of string, and work four rows of knots as shown in Diagram 1.

To finish off: Cut the loops of the grass, leaving the cut "pile" long at the bottom (ie in the foreground of the landscape), and trimming it shorter as it reaches the distant horizon. And brush up the bouclé so the sheep look really fluffy, particularly around their outlines so they overlap the grass.

If you want to have the picture framed conventionally (in which case you will need a box frame), remove it from the loom as follows: cut the warp threads at the top, as near to the tacks as possible, and tie the adjoining threads together so the knots come close to the first row of woven knots. Repeat at the bottom in the same way. Trim the warp threads short—being sure to leave at least 2 cm ($\frac{3}{4}$ in) above each knot to avoid any risk of the ends unravelling at some future date.

6
Butterflies and flowers

These brightly coloured and summery cushions will be as much fun in blazing June as when they're cheering up a bleak winter evening.

Although they look immensely complicated, our brilliant and unusual knitted cushion covers are not at all difficult to make. If you can plain and purl you're virtually there, and if you can't crochet, don't despair of success. As the cushions are backed in matching felt, you could use leftover felt to fashion the crocheted bits like butterfly bodies or the flower bobbles.

If preferred, you can knit both sides of the cushions, in which case you'll need to double the amount of wool required. But however you choose to back the cushions, you'll find it more economical to knit both versions of each design, as the two colour schemes complement one another. When finished, the flower cushions will measure about 35 cm (14 in) in diameter; the butterflies about 46 cm (18 in) at the widest point of their wingtips.

Five-colour cushions

Materials

To make two flower fronts in colour schemes A and B, you'll need Pingouin Pingofrance double knitting wool in a 25/75 wool/acrylic mixture as follows:
One 50 g (2 oz) ball each of 137 (coquelicot—a hot red), 131 (feu—a slightly darker red), 135 (poussin—a creamy yellow), 138 (orange) and 122 (rose indien—a mid-rose pink).
Two size 10 knitting needles.
A 3 mm (size 11) crochet hook.

1.2 m of 135 cm (54 in) wide cotton lining fabric for the inner cushions.

Some kapok for the stuffing. (All from
John Lewis and John Lewis Partnership stores).

1.2 m of 182 cm (72 in) of felt to match
any of the knitting wool colours, or
you could buy a smaller quantity
and back each cushion differently
(direct or mail order from The Felt
and Hessian Shop).

Method

Tension: 7 sts. and $12\frac{1}{2}$ rows to 2.5 cm
(1 in).

Abbreviations: K. = knit; P. = purl;
st. = stitch; tog. = together;
ch. = chain; s.s. = slip stitch.

Note 1. Slip the first stitch on every
row except when changing colour; knit
into the back of the stitches on the
first row to give a firm edge.

Note 2. The numbers without any
brackets around them refer to colour
scheme A; the numbers within square
brackets [ ] refer to colour scheme B.

First section: Cast on 41 sts. with 137
[138].

Rows 1 to 8: K. *9th row:* K.18, k.2
tog., k.1, k.2 tog., k.18. *10th to 12th
row:* K. *13th row:* K.17, k.2 tog., k.1,
k.2 tog., k.17. *14th to 16th row:* K. *17th
row:* K.16, k.2 tog., k.1, k.2 tog., k.16.
18th to 20th row: K. *21st row:* K.15, k.2
tog., k.1, k.2 tog., k.15.

Change colour to 131 [135]. *22nd
to 24th row:* K. *25th row:* K.14, k.2 tog.,
k.1, k.2 tog., k.14. *26th to 28th row:* K.
29th row: K.13, k.2 tog., k.1, k.2 tog.,
k.13. *30th to 32nd row:* K. *33rd row:*
K.12, k.2 tog., k.1, k.2 tog., k.12, *34th to
36th row:* K. *37th row:* K.11, k.2 tog.,
k.1, k.2 tog., k.11. *38th to 40th row:* K.
41st row: K.10, k.2 tog., k.1, k.2 tog.,
k.10.

Change colour to 122 [122]. *42nd
to 44th row:* K. *45th row:* K.9, k.2 tog.,
k.1, k.2 tog., k.9. *46th to 48th row:* K.
49th row: K.8, k.2 tog., k.1, k.2 tog.,
k.8. *50th to 52nd row:* K. *53rd row:* K.7,

k.2 tog., k.1, k.2 tog., k.7. *54th to 56th
row:* K. *57th row:* K.6, k.2 tog., k.1, k.2
tog., k.6.

Change colour to 135 [131]. *58th to
60th row:* K. *61st row:* K.5, k.2 tog., k.1,
k.2 tog., k.5.

Change colour to 122 [122]. *62nd
to 64th row:* K. *65th row:* K.4, k.2 tog.,
k.1, k.2 tog., k.4.

Change colour to 138 [137]. *66th to
68th row:* K. *69th row:* K.3, k.2 tog.,
k.1, k.2 tog., k.3. *70th to 72nd row:* K.
73rd row: K.2, k.2 tog., k.1, k.2 tog.,
k.2. *74th to 76th row:* K. *77th row:* K.1,
k.2 tog., k.1, k.2 tog., k.1. *78th to 80th
row:* K. *81st row:* K.2 tog., k.1, k.2 tog.,
82nd row: K. K.3 tog. and fasten off.

Work six more sections as for the
first section.

To make up the cushion: Either crochet or sew the sections together on
the wrong side, leaving the first eight
rows of knitting free to give a natural
petal effect.

To make the centre bobble: With
the 3 mm crochet hook, make 3 ch. and
join in a ring with s.s. *Next row:* 3 ch.,
work 14 trebles into a ring. Fasten off.

To make the inner cushion: Block
each section of the stitched-together
flower front by pinning them out round
the edges, and press lightly using a
warm iron over a damp cloth. Place
the flower front flat on a piece of
paper, draw round it, and cut out the
paper to give an exact pattern for the
inner cushion.

Using the paper pattern, cut two
pieces from the cotton lining fabric,
leaving a 1.25 cm ($\frac{1}{2}$ in) seam allowance
all round. Sew round the edges leaving
an opening. Turn through to the right
side, stuff with some of the kapok, and
sew up the opening.

To back the cushion with felt: Using
the paper pattern, cut out one flower
shape, this time without leaving any
seam allowance. Place the knitted
flower and the felt flower, wrong sides
together, and oversew all round with
tiny stitches on the right side, at the

same time inserting the kapok-stuffed inner cushion.

Finally, sew the crocheted bobble to the centre of the cushion front.

Three-colour flower cushions

Materials

To make one flower front in colour scheme C, you'll need Pingouin Pingofrance as follows:
One 50 g (2 oz) ball each of 138 (orange), 135 (poussin) and 122 (rose indien).
To make one flower front in colour scheme D, you'll need Pingouin Pingofrance as follows:
One 50 g (2 oz) each of 137 (coquelicot), 131 (feu) and 122 (rose indien).
All other requirements have already been included in the list of materials for the five-colour flower cushions.

Method

Tension: As for the five-colour flower cushions.

Note 1. As for the five-colour flower cushions.

Note 2. The numbers without any brackets around them refer to colour scheme C; the numbers within square brackets [ ] refer to colour scheme D.

First section: Cast on 25 sts. with 138 [137]. *1st to 8th row:* K. *9th row:* K.10, k.2 tog., k.1, k.2 tog., k.10. *10th to 16th row:* K. *17th row:* K.9, k.2 tog., k.1, k.2 tog., k.9. *18th to 24th row:* K. *25th row:* K.8, k.2 tog., k.1, k.2 tog., k.8. *26th to 32nd row:* K. *33rd row:* K.7, k.2 tog., k.1, k.2 tog., k.7. *34th and 35th rows:* K.

Change colour to 122 [122]. *36th to 40th row:* K. *41st row:* K.6, k.2 tog., k.1, k.2 tog., k.6. *42nd and 43rd rows:* K.

Change colour to 135 [131]. *44th to 48th row:* K. *49th row:* K.5, k.2 tog., k.1, k.2 tog., k.5. *50th to 56th row:* K. *57th row:* K.4, k.2 tog., k.1, k.2 tog., k.4. *58th to 64th row:* K. *65th row:* K.3, k.2 tog., k.1, k.2 tog., k.3. *66th to 72nd row:* K. *73rd row:* K.2, k.2 tog., k.1, k.2 tog., k.2. *74th to 79th row:* K.

Change colour to 122 [122]. *80th row:* K. *81st row:* K.1, k.2 tog., k.1, k.2 tog., k.1. *82nd to 88th row:* K. *89th row:* K.2 tog., k.1, k.2 tog. *90th row:* K.3 tog. and fasten off.

Work five more sections as for the first section. For colour scheme C, K. a further six sections using 135 (creamy yellow) in place of 138 (orange); and 138 in place of 135. For colour scheme D, K. a further six sections using 131 (feu) in place of 137 (coquelicot); and 137 in place of 131. Assemble alternately and make up in the same way as for the five-colour flower cushions.

Butterfly cushions

Materials

To make two butterfly fronts in colour schemes E and F, you'll need exactly the same amounts and colours of Pingouin Pingofrance wool as for the five-colour flower cushions.

All other requirements have already been included in the list of materials for the five-colour flower cushions.

Method

Tension and notes 1 and 2: As for the five-colour flower cushions.

To make two large five-colour wings for butterfly E: Cast on 61 sts. with 122. *1st to 8th row:* K. *9th row:* K.28, k.2 tog., k.1, k.2 tog., k.28. *10th to 12th row:* K. *13th row:* K.27, k.2 tog., k.1, k.2 tog., k.27. *14th to 16th row:* K. *17th row:* K.26, k.2 tog., k.1, k.2 tog., k.26. *18th to 20th row:* K. *21st row:* K.25, k.2 tog., k.1, k.2 tog., k.25.

Change colour to 138. *22nd to 24th row:* K. *25th row:* K.24, k.2 tog., k.1, k.2 tog., k.24. *26th to 28th row:* K. *29th row:* K.23, k.2 tog., k.1, k.2 tog., k.23. *30th to 32nd row:* K. *33rd row:* K.22, k.2 tog., k.1, k.2 tog., k.22. *34th to 36th row:* K. *37th row:* K.21, k.2 tog., k.1, k.2 tog., k.21.

Change colour to 137. *38th to 40th row:* K. *41st row:* K.20, k.2 tog., k.1, k.2

tog., k.20. *42nd to 44th row:* K. *45th row:* K.19, k.2 tog., k.1, k.2 tog., k.19. *46th to 48th row:* K. *49th row:* K.18, k.2 tog., k.1, k.2 tog., k.18. *50th to 52nd row:* K. *53rd row:* K.17, k.2 tog., k.1, k.2 tog., k.17.

Change colour to 131. *54th to 56th row:* K. *57th row:* K. 16, k.2 tog., k.1, k.2 tog., k.16. *58th to 60th row:* K. *61st row:* K.15, k.2 tog., k.1, k.2 tog., k.15. *62nd to 64th row:* K. *65th row:* K.14, k.2 tog., k.1, k.2 tog., k.14. *66th to 68th row:* K. *69th row:* K.13, k.2 tog., k.1, k.2 tog., k.13.

Change colour to 135. *70th to 72nd row:* K. *73rd row:* K.12, k.2 tog., k.1, k.2 tog., k.12. *74th to 76th row:* K. *77th row:* K.11, k.2 tog., k.1, k.2 tog., k.11. *78th to 80th row:* K. *81st row:* K.10, k.2 tog., k.1, k.2 tog., k.10. *82nd to 84th row:* K. *85th row:* K.9, k.2 tog., k.1, k.2 tog., k.9. *86th to 88th row:* K. *89th row:* K.8, k.2 tog., k.1, k.2 tog., k.8. *90th to 92nd row:* K. *93rd row:* K.7, k.2 tog., k.1, k.2 tog., k.7. *94th to 96th row:* K. *97th row:* K.6, k.2 tog., k.1, k.2 tog., k.6. *98th to 100th row:* K. *101st row:* K.5, k.2 tog., k.1, k.2 tog., k.5. *102nd to 104th row:* K. *105th row:* K.4, k.2 tog., k.1, k.2 tog., k.4. *106th to 108th row:* K. Cast off remaining 11 sts.

To make four-colour wings for butterfly F: The large wings are worked in the same way as the large wings of butterfly E, but with the following amendments:

Cast on with colour 131. *Change to colour 135* at the end of the 21st row. *Change to colour 137* at the end of the 43rd row. *Change to colour 138* at the end of the 65th row.

The small wings are worked in the same way as the small wings of butterfly E are worked, but with the following amendments:

Cast on with Colour 131. *Change to Colour 135* at the end of the 21st row. Then *change to colour 137* at the end of the 43rd row. Finally *change to colour 138* at the end of the 65th row.

To make the butterfly body for E and F: Cast on 27 sts. with 122. *1st row:* K. *2nd row:* K. into front and back of 1st st., k. to last st., k. into front and back of last st. *3rd row:* K. *4th row:* As 2nd row. *5th row:* K. *6th row:* As 2nd row. *7th to 9th row:* K. *10th row:* K.2 tog., k. to last 2 sts., k.2 tog. *11th row:* K. *12th row:* As 10th row. *13th row:* K. *14th row:* As 10th row. Cast off remaining 27 sts.

To make the butterfly head for E and F: With the 3 mm crochet hook and using 122, make 3 ch., join in a ring with s.s. *Next row:* Make 4 ch., work 17 double trebles into ring. Join with s.s. in top of 4th ch. Fasten off.

To make up the antennae for E and F: Make six lengths of ch. approximately 66 cm (26 in) in length. Plait three together neatly and evenly, thus making two cords.

To make up the cushion: Join each large wing to a small wing, lining up the inner edges (ie those next to the body), by either sewing or crocheting them together on the wrong side. This will leave the first eight rows on the small wing, and the first sixteen rows on the large wing, free to ensure that the wings look separate. Otherwise they would appear too solid for "flight". Then press lightly using a warm iron over a damp cloth.

Lay the two halves of the butterfly right sides up on a table, arranging the tips of the inner wings to touch at top and bottom. This will leave a narrow oval gap at the centre, to take the butterfly body. Catch the tips of the inner wings together at top and bottom, place the body over the oval gap, and sew securely to the wings with small, neat stitches.

Sew on the butterfly head, and stitch the antennae to the head and wings. Make the kapok-filled inner cushion and back the knitted outer cushion following the method described for the five-colour flower cushion. Now plop them onto a sofa, sit back and relax!

7

An intricately quilted bedside rug

It only takes the most basic skills to make this apparently difficult rug, where a disciplined interplay of chevron patterns lends endless textural and visual interest.

Just quilted squares joined by strips of tapestry. But this clever combination of two ordinary techniques adds up to something extraordinarily lovely. Part of the secret lies in the self- patterned chevrons; white stitching on white always looks superb. But part lies in the unexpected use of colour; the tapestry comes in soft rainbow shades. As for the amount of work involved, the chevron quilting is all done by machine and the tapestry is worked in straightforward tent stitch.

Materials

1.6 m of off-white Brough, a heavy duty cotton/linen union, 120 cm (48 ins) wide.

1.3 m of medium-weight Terylene wadding, 90 cm (36 ins) wide.

1.3 m of white muslin, 90 cm (36 ins) wide. (All from John Lewis and branches of the John Lewis Partnership.

1.3 m of white tapestry canvas, 68 cm (27 ins) wide, with 12 holes to the inch.

Anchor stranded cottons as follows: 29 skeins of 0402; 15 of 0160; 16 of 0301; 14 of 050.

Method

To make the quilted squares: Cut out fifteen 25 cm (10 in) squares from the Brough fabric, the Terylene wadding and the muslin. Taking one of each, lay the wadding on top of the muslin, and the Brough on top, right side up. Pin together round the edges. On each of the fifteen squares, pin-mark a stepping diagonal line, 2.5 cm (1 in) across, and 2.5 cm (1 in) down, from the top left corner to bottom right. Machine-stitch the line.

NB This stepping diagonal line is the only one you'll need to make the four different chevron patterns. It's the spacing between the lines that creates the difference.

For the narrow chevron: You will need to make three squares. Using a wide zigzag foot, and with the edge of the foot against your first stepping diagonal line, machine another stepping diagonal line. Always keeping the edge of the foot against the previous line, continue to machine lines above—and then below—the original line, until you have finally filled up the whole square.

For the medium chevron: You will need to make four squares. Machine as before, but this time, space the stepping diagonal lines 1.5 cm ($\frac{5}{8}$ in) apart. It may help to pin-mark the first few lines, but then you can machine by eye to fill the squares as they don't have to be 100% accurate.

For the wide chevron: Make four squares as follows:

Machine a line only half a machine-foot away from the first diagonal stepping line. Repeat this pair of closely spaced lines at wide, 2.5 cm (1 in) intervals until you have filled up the square in its entirety.

For the squared chevron: Make four squares as follows:

Machine a line only half a machine-foot away from the first diagonal stepping line. Work the next line above so that the downward steps just touch the corners of the first pair of stepping lines, to form squares. Work the next line above only half a machine-foot away, to make the pair. Repeat the process continually until you have filled the whole square.

To make the tapestry strips: Lay the tapestry canvas on a table with the selvedges running from left to right. Against the top edge, draw in pencil two strips each of 128 cm (50¼ in) by 5.5 cm (2¼ in). Parallel to them, draw two strips each of 82 cm (32¼ in) by 5.5 cm (2¼ in). Parallel to them, draw four strips each of 77 cm (30¼ in) by 5.5 cm (2¼ in). On the remaining canvas, draw ten strips each of 26 cm (10¼ in) by 5.5 cm (2¼ in). Cut out all strips carefully.

On each strip of canvas, a seam allowance of 1.5 cm ($\frac{5}{8}$ in) on either side and at both ends has been allocated. This leaves you a central strip, just 12 holes wide, to work in tapestry. On all the canvas strips, draw in pencil these central strips for guidance.

Using tent stitch (see the diagram on page 66 if you need a reference), work the central strips with stripes of colour as follows: 7 rows of blue; 5 of white; 7 of yellow; 5 of white; 7 of pink; 5 of white. Repeat the stripes for the length of the central strips.

When completed, pin out the strips, right side down, onto a board, pulling out any twist in the canvas. Steam-iron, but without pressing down on the canvas, and leave to dry.

To make up the rug: Trim all the quilted squares to 23 cm (9 in) square. Arrange them on the floor as in the photograph, so that all the diagonal stepping lines run from top left to bottom right, and each of the four chevron patterns forms a diagonal line across the rug.

Begin by joining the squares into threes, to give five vertical rows. Using the 26 cm (10¼ in) strips of tapestry horizontally, machine them to the squares with right sides together, working from the strip side so that you can machine really tight up against the line of tapestry stitches. Press all the seam allowances open.

Next, join the five resulting rows together, using the 77 cm (30¼ in) strips of tapestry vertically between them. Make sure the short horizontal strips match on either side of the long vertical strips. Again, press all the seam allowances open.

To finish the edges of the rug, machine one 128 cm (50¼ in) strip to each long side of the rug, and one 82 cm (32¼ in) strip to each short side of the rug. Press seam allowances open.

To back the rug: Cut from the Brough fabric a 128 cm (50¼ in) by 82 cm (32¼ in) rectangle to form the backing. With right sides together, and leaving a 1.5 cm ($\frac{5}{8}$ in) seam allowance, machine the backing fabric all around the edge from the rug side, so that the machine-stitches come tight up against the tapestry stitches.

Leave a 50 cm (19½ in) gap at one of the short ends of the rug. Trim all the seam allowances, and then turn the rug right side out. Next, hand-sew the 50 cm (19½ in) gap together as neatly and invisibly as possible.

With your fingers, press the edges of the rug so that the backing fabric is just out of sight. Pin to hold in position, and then machine all around the rug from the right side, so the stitches disappear into the "crack" of the seam where the tapestry edging strip joins the quilted squares.

Finally, pin and then machine down the "cracks" of the seams where the 77 cm (30¼ in) vertical strips of tapestry join the quilted squares.

8

All dressed in white

The bride only wears her dress for a day, but this beautifully covered and decorated album will always be a reminder of the big occasion.

Endless care goes into preparing weddings, but the photograph album receives little attention. So we've devised one that will be worthy of the great day. It will be even more worthy if it incorporates scraps from the bride's and bridesmaids' dresses.

Materials

A 35 cm ($13\frac{3}{4}$ in) by 30 cm ($11\frac{3}{4}$ in) photograph album (from larger branches of Boots).

0.5 m of 90 cm (36 in) wide white velvet.

0.5 m of 90 cm (36 in) wide lightweight iron-on Vilene.

0.6 cm of 10 cm (4 in) wide white satin ribbon for the spine.

3 m of 1.5 ($\frac{5}{8}$ in) wide white satin ribbon for the binding.

2.5 m of 6 mm ($\frac{1}{4}$ in) wide pink ribbon for the lettering.

Pink thread to match.

Scraps of fabric for the appliqued flowers and leaves.

Machine embroidery thread to match.

A tube of Copydex glue.

Dewhurst's dressmakers' tracing paper.

Tracing paper. (All from John Lewis and John Lewis Partnership stores.)

Miniature glass beads and a beading needle (from Ells & Farrier, or mail order from Creative Beadcraft. Minimum order 25 g (1 oz) on most beads).

Method

Cut the velvet and Vilene to measure

88 cm (35 in) by 39.7 cm ($15\frac{5}{8}$ in). Place the Vilene shiny side down on the wrong side of the velvet, cover with a clean cloth, and iron with the setting on cotton. Tack a vertical line down the centre of the Vilene-backed velvet, and then tack a parallel line 5 cm (2 in) to the right. This parallel line marks the left edge of the front cover.

To mark the remaining three edges of the front cover, tack lines 4 cm ($1\frac{1}{2}$ in) down from the top, 4 cm ($1\frac{1}{2}$ in) up from the bottom and 8 cm (3 in) in from the right. These tacked lines make a "frame" into which to fit your "picture" of flowers, leaves and lettering, as shown in Diagram 1.

To applique the flowers and leaves: Next, draw the measurements of the "frame" onto the ordinary tracing paper, and using the photograph as a guide, draw on the flower and leaf shapes and the lettering. Place the dressmakers' tracing paper, ink side down, on the scraps of fabric and put the ordinary tracing paper on top. Using a ballpoint pen, transfer the outlines of the flower and leaf shapes to the fabric, and cut out. Arrange the shapes on the velvet and using a matching thread, tack them in place with small stitches. Machine around the shapes with small, close zigzag stitches to cover the raw edges.

To add the lettering: Take the ordinary tracing paper, and make pinholes through the traced outline of the lettering, about 1.25 cm ($\frac{1}{2}$ in) apart. Lay the tracing paper accurately on the appliqued velvet, and make dot marks through the pinholes with a soft pencil. Cut an end of pink ribbon on the slant and lay at the beginning of the first letter. Follow the lines of the letter with the ribbon, twisting it over on curves and corners, and pinning as you go. Cut off the ribbon on the slant at the end of the letter.

Working one letter at a time, tack the ribbon edges, remove the pins, and slipstitch neatly into place. When com-

pleted, press from the wrong side.

To make the satin spine: Cut a 31 cm ($12\frac{1}{2}$ in) length of the 10 cm (4 in) wide ribbon. Tack it into position as shown in Diagram 2, so that the right edge of the ribbon just covers the tacking stitches on the left of the "picture"; and so that it stops slightly short of the top and bottom of the "frame". Carefully machine all round the edges of the ribbon with small, close zigzag stitches. Press from the wrong side.

To make the satin corners: Cut two identical triangles from the 10 cm (4 in) wide satin ribbon, so that the longest side measures 12.5 cm (5 in) and the other two sides each measure 8.6 cm ($3\frac{3}{8}$ in). Lay them in position as shown in Diagram 2, so that the two shorter sides each project 6 mm ($\frac{1}{4}$ in) beyond the "frame". Machine with small, close zigzag stitches around all three sides.

To complete the basic cover: First, work the beaded flowers, referring to the photograph for guidance. The glass beads come in a generous selection of colours, so you'll have no difficulty relating them to whatever coloured fabrics you've used. Then, 1 cm ($\frac{3}{8}$ in) in from the sides of the satin spine, cut down about 4.5 cm ($1\frac{3}{4}$ in), or as near to the zigzag stitching at the top and bottom of the spine as you can go without cutting through it. Zigzag neaten the edges of the resulting centre flaps. Fold the 1.5 cm ($\frac{5}{8}$ in) wide satin ribbon in half lengthways and press. Use it to bind all the raw edges with the exception of the centre flaps by folding the ribbon over the raw edge, tacking and machining. There's no need to be meticulous about mitring the corners, as these will be trimmed off when you come to make the sleeves.

To fit the cover to the album: Make sleeves for the album to slip into as shown in Diagram 3. Fold in the right and left edges of the cover by 8 cm (3 in), so right sides of the velvet are together. Pin, and then machine across the 8 cm (3 in) fold, 4 cm ($1\frac{1}{2}$ in) below

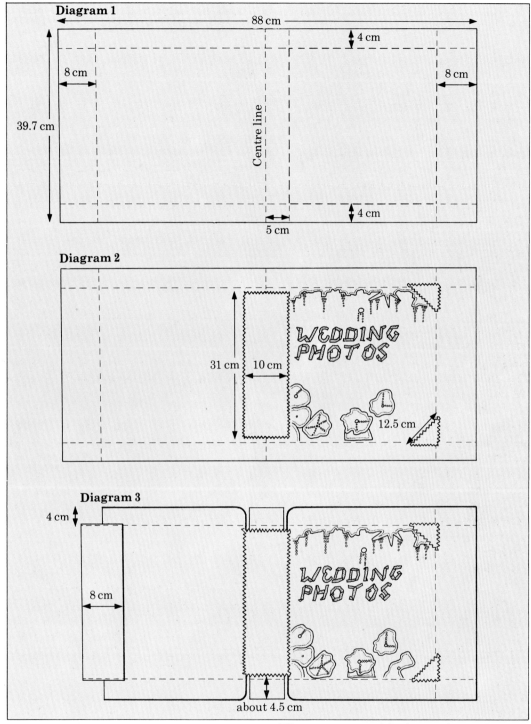

Diagram 1

88 cm

4 cm

8 cm

Centre line

8 cm

39.7 cm

5 cm

4 cm

Diagram 2

31 cm 10 cm

WEDDING PHOTOS

12.5 cm

Diagram 3

4 cm

8 cm

WEDDING PHOTOS

about 4.5 cm

the top edge and above the bottom edge. Trim the folded-in 8 cm (3 in) of velvet to within 6 mm ($\frac{1}{4}$ in) of the machine stitching, but only trim the corresponding 8 cm (3 in) underneath to halfway along the machine stitching.

Then turn outside in, to form sleeves inside the velvet cover.

To finish off, glue the centre flaps inside the spine, and glue the satin ribbon bound edges securely to the inside of the front and back covers.

9

A picture of domestic bliss

This charming collage of a miniature bedroom is complete right down to the wooden skirting. You could copy it, or adapt the design to reproduce your real-life bedroom.

One of the beauties of this appealing design is that you can simplify it if you're short of time. Our version has a tent-stitched tapestry carpet, but you could easily glue on a "carpet" instead. An off-cut of heavy fabric would be ideal—something like moquette or a printed velvet. Or you could even stick on an actual piece of carpet provided it wasn't too thick for the job.

You could make a simpler bedspread too, using any lightweight tiny-patterned printed fabric like a Liberty Tana lawn or a Laura Ashley cotton. This could really be fun if you use a leftover from a fabric actually used in your bedroom. With luck you'll find plenty of suitable bits and pieces just by rummaging through the collection in your scrap bag.

Materials

The patchwork quilt

A 9.5 mm ($\frac{3}{8}$ in) hexagonal "window" template; if you're a beginner, a leaflet with full sewing instructions by Quiltery (from good craft or art-needlework shops). Scraps of any lightweight tiny-patterned cotton or silk fabric.

A piece of 14 cm ($5\frac{1}{2}$ in) by 16 cm ($6\frac{1}{4}$ in) plain white lawn or finely woven cotton, to form a backing.

A piece of 14 cm ($5\frac{1}{2}$ in) by 16 cm ($6\frac{1}{4}$ in) Terylene wadding to plump up the patchwork so it looks fat and three-dimensional.

Other bed-linen

A scrap of embroidered white cotton for the pillowcases. We used a piece from an old nightdress, but broderie anglaise would do as well—or you could use plain white cotton.

A small piece of Terylene wadding to fatten the pillows.

A scrap of white cotton for the sheet.

Bedstead and other woodwork

Some balsa wood.

Some balsa cement.

A craft knife (all from model shops or large art shops).

A 125 ml ($4\frac{1}{2}$ oz) tin of Rustins Matt Wood Stain (from most D.I.Y. shops).

Home Sweet Home sampler

A small off-cut of tapestry canvas with 24 holes to the inch.

Anchor stranded embroidery cotton in colour reference 022.

Tapestry carpet

A piece of tapestry canvas measuring 23 cm (9 in) by 13 cm (5 in) with 16 holes to the inch.

Anchor tapisserie wools in 0421, 0564, 071, 0498, 068 and 0358.

A packet of Milwards size 18–24 tapestry needles (they're not available for sale individually).

Window and curtains

Some mid-blue coloured card to suggest sky (from art shops).

A scrap of lace or net, about 8 cm (3 in) wide by 10 cm (4 in) deep.

A piece of lightweight, small-patterned cotton fabric, 8 cm (3 in) wide by 13 cm ($5\frac{1}{4}$ in) deep, for the curtains.

A piece of matching fabric 8 cm (3 in) wide by 2.5 cm (1 in) deep, with selvedge running along the bottom width, for the pelmet. (If there's no selvedge, cut the piece 3 cm ($1\frac{1}{4}$ in) deep to allow for a narrow hem.)

Walls

A 21 cm ($8\frac{1}{2}$ in) by 27 cm ($10\frac{1}{2}$ in) piece of any small-patterned fabric or paper. (We used an off-cut of actual wallpaper.)

A miniature tin of Humbrol gloss to paint the skirting board (from model shops).

For overall

A 21 cm ($8\frac{1}{2}$ in) by 27 cm ($10\frac{1}{2}$ in) piece of plain card upon which to stick the collage (from art shops).

A tube of Copydex glue.

Method

How to make the bedding: Work the patchwork quilt; you'll find you need 59 patches. When you have sewn them together, centre them on the 14 cm ($5\frac{1}{2}$ in) by 16 cm ($6\frac{1}{4}$ in) plain white fabric, and neatly applique the patchwork to the backing.

Next, lay the backed patchwork, face down, on the 14 cm ($5\frac{1}{2}$ in) by 16 cm ($6\frac{1}{4}$ in) piece of Terylene wadding. Machine-stitch the sides and bottom 1 cm ($\frac{3}{8}$ in) in from the edges. Trim any excess wadding and turn the completed quilt right sides out.

NB If you're using a piece of real carpet instead of doing the tapestry, it's best to use two thicknesses of the Terylene wadding to allow for the extra bulk of the carpet.

Now take the scrap of white cotton for the sheet, and cut a piece measuring 14 cm ($5\frac{1}{2}$ in) wide by 4 cm ($1\frac{1}{2}$ in) long. Fold the 4 cm ($1\frac{1}{2}$ in) long edges under by 6 mm ($\frac{1}{4}$ in) and iron flat. Lay the sheet, wrong side up, across the top of the right side of the quilt. Machine the two together 1.25 cm ($\frac{1}{2}$ in) down from the top. Turn the sheet over to the wrong side of the quilt—this will leave 1.25 cm ($\frac{1}{2}$ in) of sheet showing on the right side—and tack into position.

To make the pillows, cut four 7 cm ($2\frac{3}{4}$ in) by 4.5 cm ($1\frac{3}{4}$ in) pieces from the scrap of white embroidered, or plain, cotton. Place two of the pieces right sides together, and machine around three of the sides 6 mm ($\frac{1}{4}$ in) from edge.

Turn the right way out, iron the pillowcase and stuff it with Terylene wadding. Fold in the raw edges on the remaining side, and neatly oversew. Make the other pillow in same way.

How to make the bedstead: Referring to the photograph for guidance, cut strips from the balsa wood using the craft knife. Arrange the strips on a piece of paper and when satisfied with the result, stick into position with the balsa cement. Cut away the surplus paper and stain the bedstead with the wood dye. Or of course, you could leave the bedstead unstained if you wanted a lighter finish, and simply give it a coat of clear varnish.

How to make the sampler: Cut a piece of white paper measuring 6 cm ($2\frac{3}{8}$ in) wide by 5 cm ($1\frac{7}{8}$ in) long. This will provide a backing for the sampler, so the wallpaper doesn't show through in the completed collage. Referring to the photograph for guidance, and using the small scraps of 24 hole-to-the-inch canvas and the Anchor stranded cotton, work the Home Sweet Home lettering and the border in cross-stitch. Next, squeeze a little Copydex onto the edges of the piece of paper, and stick the canvas onto the paper, making sure to centre it so the border of the sampler runs parallel to the edges of the paper. When dry, trim away the excess canvas so the sampler is the same size as the paper.

Now cut four strips of balsa wood, to make a frame with outer measurements of 6 cm ($2\frac{3}{8}$ in) wide by 5 cm ($1\frac{7}{8}$ in) long. Stain with wood dye, and when dry, stick the strips of balsa wood onto the sampler, using the balsa cement.

How to make the carpet: Take the piece of 16 hole-to-the-inch canvas, measuring 23 cm (9 in) wide by 13 cm (5 in) long. Turn the edges in by 1.2 cm ($\frac{1}{2}$ in), press in position and tack.

Following the pattern in the photograph stitch by stitch, and using the tapisserie wools, work the tapestry in tent stitch (see page 66), continuing it for 6 mm ($\frac{1}{4}$ in) under each side of where the bed will go. If you find the tapestry is off-square when you've finished it, straighten it as follows. Pin a piece of graph paper to a drawing board or pastry board and place the tapestry face down onto it. Dampen the back of tapestry, and using the lines on the graph paper as a guide, pin it firmly to the wooden board, pulling it square as you go. Leave the tapestry to dry naturally before unpinning, by which time its lines should be true again.

NB If you're using a fabric for the carpet, cut it to the same size as the tapestry canvas, and turn under and tack the same amount all around. If you're using an off-cut of actual carpet, there'll be no need to turn the edges, so cut it 1.25 cm ($\frac{1}{2}$ in) smaller than the tapestry canvas all round.

How to make the curtain and pelmet: Take the small piece of patterned curtain fabric, turn the sides under 2 mm ($\frac{1}{8}$ in) and machine-stitch. Turn under the bottom by 1 cm ($\frac{3}{8}$ in) and either machine-stitch or hem by hand. Take the small piece of pelmet fabric, and turn under all but the selvedge edge by 6 mm ($\frac{1}{4}$ in) and iron flat. If you do not have a selvedge, also turn under the bottom edge by 2 mm ($\frac{1}{8}$ in) and iron flat.

To assemble the collage: Whether you're using a paper or a fabric, glue your "wallpaper" to the same-size piece of plain card with Copydex. Then, lining the bottom edge of the carpet up with the bottom edge of the card, stick the carpet into place over the lower part of the wallpaper.

Now make the skirting board, by cutting a piece of balsa wood about 20 cm (8 in) by 1.25 cm ($\frac{1}{2}$ in), and painting it in a co-ordinating Humbrol paint colour. When dry, fix it in place so it butts tightly against the top of the carpet, using the balsa cement.

Using Copydex, stick the patchwork quilt into position; and then add the pillows, sticking just the lower halves into position. This will allow you greater leeway when you come to fix the bedhead above them. If, as you position the pillows ready for glueing, any unwanted wallpaper shows through the gap between them, stick a piece of white paper under the pillows to form an undersheet.

Stick the bedstead into position with Copydex, allowing the bedhead to extend down behind the pillows very slightly. Stick the sampler into place with Copydex.

Finally, work the window. Cut a 5 cm (2 in) wide by 10 cm (4 in) deep piece from the mid-blue coloured card. Taking your piece of lace or net, make a 1.25 cm ($\frac{1}{2}$ in) fold along one of the 10 cm (4 in) sides, and stick it to the reverse of the card along its right-hand 10 cm (4 in) side. Stick the blue card onto the top right-hand corner of the collage, so that the glued edge of the lace is at the right-hand side of the window. Now lightly iron the lace into realistic folds, and stick into position at the top and left-hand side of the card, leaving the folds to hang naturally at the bottom.

Lightly iron the curtain and pelmet, and stick the curtain into position first, so it just covers the edge of the lace or net. Then stick the pelmet on straight, and your Home Sweet Home collage is finished at last.

An easy eggshell finish for Easter

**There's no mystique about making these
Easter eggs. They're simple enough for
a child to tackle, and they'll give
pleasure out of all proportion to the
minimal efforts put in.**

Our Easter eggs are bright and cheerful, with deliberately crude and naive designs expressed in strong and punchy colours. That's why we could use crayons and felt-tipped pens—more delicate designs with subtle shading would require the use of paints and brushes. See page 121 for alternative suggestions, including edible eggs that don't need "blowing". But now for this zippy and colourful clutch.

Materials

Some eggs—preferably free-range farm
  eggs, as these tend to have stronger
  shells.
A pin.
A matchstick.
Felt-tipped pens or wax crayons.
Clear varnish (from art shops—or you
  could use clear nail varnish).

Method

To blow out the contents: Take an egg, and hold it in one hand with the bottom end resting on a firm surface. Push gently with a pin until you have made a tiny prick in the top end. Do this very carefully, as you can crack the egg just by concentrating too hard on making the hole, or by holding the egg too tightly. Turn the egg the other way round, and pierce another hole in the other end. Make one of the holes larger by working in a matchstick cautiously, and then push the matchstick through until you have managed to break the yolk inside the shell.

Holding the egg over a plate, blow through the small pinprick and the liquid will trickle out through the larger hole. Now rinse out the shell and let it dry naturally. If the big hole gapes a bit, you can fill it with a dab of fine Polyfilla.

To decorate the eggs: Holding the eggshell very gently, begin colouring in whatever design you fancy. If you're nervous about your artistic abilities, stick to bold stripes, dots and zigzags— they're simple yet effective. But you'll be surprised how easy it is to achieve more ambitious effects, particularly as with felt-tipped pens and crayons— as opposed to a paint brush—you have total control over the movements you make. Our Easter chick emerging from its "broken" shell, for instance, is well within even the most diffident person's capabilities.

If you're working in felt-pen, when you've finished one side (or one colour) it's best to leave the egg to dry for a while, or the work may smudge. And do try to keep your hands clean and dry throughout—otherwise you may leave fingerprints behind you.

When the decorated egg is completed (make sure it's dry if you've been using felt-pen), finish it with a light layer of clear varnish. This will make the colours brighter and give a sheen to any uncoloured eggshell. It will also make the eggs stronger.

11

A very special valentine

Although it looks a real labour of love, this sumptuously rich and detailed Valentine is fairly quick and easy to make. In fact, its chiefly a matter of sticking in pins.

Jokey cards aren't good enough for someone you love, and even pretty and romantic shop-bought cards lack the intimacy of a hand-made message. But this plump and fulsome velvet heart harks back to more sentimental days. It's inspired by the ones sailors used to make at sea to give to their sweethearts when they reached dry land. Their versions were more elaborate than ours. They padded and appliqued shapes upon shapes, sometimes basing their designs upon a star, and building up a kaleidoscope of pattern. And then they began adding the ornamentation, pinning beads through sequins as we have here.

Sailors, of course, had endless hours to kill, especially when the seas were becalmed. On the basis that you'll be in more of a hurry, we've evolved a simpler, non-appliqued Valentine, that still looks decoratively rich and detailed. By using just pins, pearl beads and mother of pearl sequins, the result is subtle, soft and romantic, and the dull, matt-textured velvet sets it off well. We used Lister's Westminster velvet in Porcelain Blue, but their unusual Walnut and Regency Cream colours would also make a perfect background for the glowing irridescence of the mother of pearl.

If you haven't got a sweetheart, but long to start a pin cushion, they make ideal commemorative gifts, and you can easily evolve designs for different

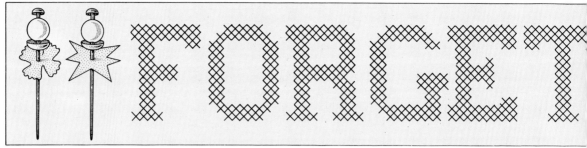

situations, based on a square or rect-angular shape. A white satin-covered cushion, decorated with just pearls and pins, would make a most appealing christening present with the name and birth-date of the baby worked into the pattern. And a yellow silk-covered cushion, decorated with the very same beads and sequins we've used, but in the gold colour which is also available, would make a spectacular gift for a golden wedding anniversary. The possibilities for birthdays and anniversaries are endless—but back to commemorating St. Valentine's Day.

Materials

0.5 m of 100% cotton pile velvet.

A reel of matching thread.

1.4 kg (3 lb) of sawdust (from pet shops or timber yards).

A box of Lils pins (ie small pins).

A box of ordinary size dressmaking pins.

1.5 m of matching or white narrow lampshade trimming.

$100 \times$ SS19/4 star-shaped plastic sequins in mother of pearl.

$100 \times$ SS22/4 flower-shaped plastic sequins in mother of pearl.

$100 \times$ SS15/4 leaf-shaped plastic sequins in mother of pearl.

$100 \times$ SS18/4 shell-shaped plastic sequins in mother of pearl.

$10 \times$ SS223/4 large flower-shaped plastic sequins in mother of pearl—this is the minimum number that can be ordered.

700×2 mm-diameter imitation pearl beads.

$100 \times 2\frac{1}{2}$ mm-diameter imitation pearl beads.

$300 \times 3\frac{1}{2}$ mm-diameter imitation pearl beads.

$1 \times$ string of CS5/4 plastic cup sequins in mother of pearl—the minimum order of one string comprises about 1000 cup sequins.

(All sequins and pearls direct from Ells & Farrier Ltd; or mail order from Creative Beadcraft Ltd.)

NB With the exception of the large flowers and the cup sequins, all sequins and pearls have to be ordered to the nearest hundred—which means there's a minimum order of one hundred. Do remember to quote reference numbers where applicable, to avoid any possible confusion.

Method

First of all, make a paper heart pattern. The heart measures 40 cm ($15\frac{3}{4}$ in) at its widest; 37 cm ($14\frac{1}{2}$ in) at its longest. If you're afraid your pattern may be lopsided, fold the paper in half, and marking it only 20 cm (8 in) wide, cut out both sides in one go.

Fold the velvet in half, pin on the paper pattern and cut out—giving you the front and back of your heart. Decide which piece is to be back, and make a vertical 10 cm (4 in) cut in the centre. (You'll need this to push the sawdust through when it's time to stuff the heart.)

Now take both front and back of heart, and with right sides of the velvet together, tack and machine round 1 cm ($\frac{3}{8}$ in) from the edge, leaving a 10 cm (4 in) gap. Using very sharp scissors, make a series of cuts round the edge, about 1 cm ($\frac{3}{8}$ in) apart, stop-

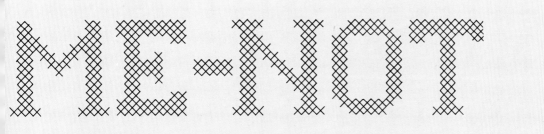

ping as close to the machine stitches as is possible without actually cutting through them. Turn the heart right sides out and hand-stitch up the gap.

To stuff, push sawdust through the vertical 10 cm (4 in) cut that you made earlier in the back of the heart. You will need to really force the sawdust in, as the plumper the result, the better it will be. The blunt end of a knitting needle is ideal for pushing the sawdust right through to the point of the heart. When you can't force any more sawdust in, sew up the cut firmly.

To decorate the heart: Trace the FORGET-ME-NOT lettering on this page onto fine tissue paper, and pin the tissue paper into position on the front of the heart. Every cross in the lettering represents a 2 mm-diameter pearl bead. To fix the pearls, stick the tiny Lils pins through them. Once all the pearls have been pinned in position, tear the tissue paper away carefully, using a needle.

To underline the lettering, we alternated flower and star sequins, plus cup sequins and $3\frac{1}{2}$ mm-diameter pearl beads. We fixed them in position with the ordinary dressmaking pins, as shown in the illustration above, in the left-hand corner of the page. If you have difficulty keeping the sequins straight and evenly spaced, it might be worth marking a strip of paper with the spacing, and pinning it just below where the row of sequins is to come, to provide a useful guide.

Now cut a small heart out of tissue paper, and use it as a guide for the heart with the date in. We outlined this heart with cup sequins plus $2\frac{1}{2}$ mm-diameter pearl beads, fixed with Lils pins. We also used $2\frac{1}{2}$ mm-diameter pearls for the date. But of course, you could easily adapt the design—you could put your name rather than the date, for instance.

By now you should have "got your eye in" enough to make the big outer heart shape without much difficulty. We used the same combination of flower and star sequins, plus cup sequins and $3\frac{1}{2}$ mm pearls, as we used to underline the Forget-Me-Not lettering. Again, you could mark a strip of paper with the spacing if the distance between the sequins begins to vary.

Adding the final details: Once you have established these basic shapes, it's up to you how much decoration you create around them. Provided you keep it strictly symmetrical, and stick to just pins and mother of pearl sequins, the results are bound to prove successful. Using the ordinary dressmaking pins, we added wing shapes of leaf sequins either side of the small heart, and scattered a few flowers within its point, made up of flower sequins, cup sequins and $2\frac{1}{2}$ mm pearls. We used pins and shell sequins at the centre-top of the big heart, and then made bold circles either side, with the large mother of pearl flower sequins at their centre, and rings of leaf and shell sequins radiating out. The lampshade trimming provided the finishing touch. Simply pinned into position through some of the leftover pearls, this hid the seam in a neat and attractive way. But as you'll probably have lots of spare sequins and beads, there's plenty of scope for ingenuity.

12-22

Preserved to perfection

One of the pleasures of making preserves is that they live long enough to justify handsome presentation. You can admire them for months with satisfaction.

Imagine opening the store cupboard door and seeing a miniature Fortnum and Mason. There's nothing like an array of homemade preserves to fill you with a sense of richness and bounty. And as it takes little extra time to make more than you need, you have a source of truly luxurious gifts. Friends who live alone, and who don't cook because making small quantities is dispiriting, will be thrilled to receive one of these luscious goodies. Now for how to make our eleven preserves, and suggestions for how to package them prettily. *All teaspoonfuls are level unless otherwise specified.*

12 Spiced oranges
Like the spiced apricots on page 105, these make a delicious extra to go with a cold bacon joint or ham. You could serve them straight from the jar at the table.

Ingredients

6 oranges.
900 ml (1½ pints) of white vinegar.
700 g (1½ lb) of white sugar.
½ stick of cinnamon broken into two pieces.
A few cloves.

Method

Scrub the oranges and discard the tops and bottoms. Cut into rings, and simmer in just enough water to cover for about 45 minutes, or until the rind

is soft. Add the vinegar, sugar and cloves. When the sugar has dissolved, bring to the boil, and continue boiling until the syrup begins to thicken. Cool and pack into jars. If the cloves stay on top, distribute them evenly throughout the oranges; pop in the cinnamon and seal immediately.

Although spiced oranges don't need to be sterilised, they look very good in a spring top jar. But any wide-necked clear glass jar would do. We tied a bow of grass green ribbon round the top, and stuck on a large green-edged self-adhesive label. The labels are available at most big stationers.

13 Preserved pork paté

This makes a marvellous start to a meal, but it's substantial enough for a light lunch. Eat within a week.

Ingredients

450 g (1 lb) of lean pork.
450 g (1 lb) of pigs liver.
450 g (1 lb) of good sausage meat.
A small glass of sherry or wine.
1 clove of garlic.
10 juniper berries.
2.5 ml ($\frac{1}{2}$ teaspoonful) of ground mace.
10 black peppercorns, roughly crushed.
1 teaspoonful of thyme.
A pinch of salt.

Method

Mince the pork and liver and mix in a bowl with the other ingredients. Put in a greased loaf tin or terrine, and arrange a couple of bay leaves on top. Stand the tin or terrine in a shallow pan of water, and bake an hour in the oven at 180°C (375°F) gas mark 5. When cooked, pack paté tightly into wide necked preserving jars, and cover with a layer of melted butter. Seal, and place in a pan of water to just below the neck of the jars. Bring to simmering point on top of the cooker and maintain for an hour. Remove the jars and cool them. If using one of the new Kilner jars, take off the orange screw-band, because it seriously limits the scope of presentation. We tied a narrow beige tape round the top of our jar, and threaded onto it an ordinary cream luggage label, which we first cut down to suitable proportions. Finally, we wrote on the inscription, in italic writing using a thick-nib pen. Even if calligraphy is not your strong point, any lettering looks more impressive than thin, scribbly biro.

14 Lemons in olive oil

The lemon-flavoured oil is ideal for making salad dressings, and you can use the lemon chopped up in salads.

Ingredients

4 whole and unpeeled scrubbed lemons.
1 unpeeled lemon sliced vertically in half.
Some good olive oil.
A few cloves.

Method

Stick four cloves in each lemon, and place in any clear glass jar with a wide neck and a tight-fitting lid. Cover with olive oil and leave for a month.

Clear glass is essential so the lemons can be seen. They look so decorative in their own right, all they really need is a bold, simple label. We used a blue-edged self-adhesive label, and again, wrote on it with a thick-nib pen.

15 Grapefruit marmalade

This is a jelly marmalade made with small, thin strips of peel. You can make it at any time of the year.

Ingredients

1.4 kg (3 lb) of grapefruit.
225 g ($\frac{1}{2}$ lb) of lemons.
3.4 litres (6 pints) of water.
2.8 kg (6 lb) of white sugar.

Method

Scrub the fruit and peel it finely with a potato peeler. Snip the peel into slim shreds and put in a saucepan with half the water. Simmer covered for 2 hours until the peel is soft. Chop the fruit into chunks and put in another saucepan with the rest of the water. Cover and simmer for $1\frac{1}{2}$ hours. Strain the fruit pulp through a fine sieve and add the strained liquid to the peel. Bring to the boil and reduce slightly before adding warmed sugar. Bring up to a fast boil and boil rapidly until set. As soon as the peel has suspended, pour into jars, top at once with waxed discs and cover with cellophane.

The light shines right through this clear marmalade, so be sure to use a glass container. We used a hexagon-shaped ex-mustard jar and covered it in a small white paper doily. If you buy the tiny doilys meant for coasters, you'll find they fit small jars ideally. The solid centres will hide everything underneath completely, while the edges will provide a frill at the sides that doesn't entail any fiddly cutting to size. We secured the doily with a rubber band and then hid the band with a narrow, knotted, brown velvet ribbon. A brown-edged self-adhesive label repeated the colour.

16 Pickled mushrooms

These make an excellent accompaniment to a dish of cold meats, but they're also good with grilled meat.

Ingredients

1.2 kg (2 to 3 lb) of button mushrooms.
1.1 litres (2 pints) of white vinegar (or malt if preferred).
13 g ($\frac{1}{2}$ oz) of allspice.
13 g ($\frac{1}{2}$ oz) of whole cloves.
13 g ($\frac{1}{2}$ oz) of cinnamon.
13 g ($\frac{1}{2}$ oz) of white pepper.
13 g ($\frac{1}{2}$ oz) of root ginger.
13 g ($\frac{1}{2}$ oz) of whole coriander.

Method

Make some spiced vinegar by adding all the spices to the vinegar, bringing to the boil, and simmering for half an hour. Cut the mushroom stalks flush with the gills, and place in a saucepan with a sprinkling of salt. Heat gently until the juices run and evaporate. Pack the mushrooms into any jars with vinegar-proof screw top lids, and pour over the cold spiced vinegar.

Our jar originally held stem ginger. We covered the lid with a patterned fabric that looks crisply appetising, and this time used a grey-edged label.

17 Sweet pickled onions

These are perfect eat   v h cold meats and cheese. The c   olour.

Ingredients

450 g (1 lb) of picklir
600 ml (1 pint) of wh   .ar.
225 g ($\frac{1}{2}$ lb) of sugar.
1 stem of root ginger.
4 green/red fresh chillies.
A handful of black and white peppercorns.
A few bayleaves.

Method

Place the onions in boiling water for two minutes. Drain, and discard brown outer skins. Boil the vinegar with the sugar and add the spices. Pack the onions in a jar, arranging the chillies and bayleaves so they show to good advantage. Pour over the vinegar, cover and seal, and leave for a month.

The pickled onions, plus the flamboyant chillies, make such a dramatic visual impact they're best left free to speak for themselves. Use any wide glass jar with a spring top or vinegar proof screw top, and add just a simple label. You could use one of the self-adhesive stationers' labels, edged in a no-nonsense band of colour. Or like us (see label in the foreground), you could cut an oval shape from white paper, draw a coloured line round the inside edge and stick on the jar with a dab of Gloy. An oval plastic template, from most big stationers, could help you get the shape right.

18 Lemon thyme jelly

Although this recipe uses lemon thyme, you could use mint, tarragon, or almost any herb from your garden. And you could make a gooseberry jelly base instead of apple. Whichever version you prefer, it will go well with game and most roast meats.

Ingredients

1.8 kg (4 lb) of cooking apples.
1.7 litres (3 pints) of water.
700 g ($1\frac{1}{2}$ lb) of sugar.
Some sprigs of lemon thyme.

Method

Cut up the apples, pips and all, and put in a saucepan with the water. Add a few sprigs of lemon thyme. Bring to the boil and simmer until the apple is very soft. Strain through a jelly bag. Pour the strained juice into a saucepan, add warmed sugar, and once dissolved, boil rapidly until a set is reached. Remove any scum, and add a few leaves of finely-chopped lemon thyme. Pour into small pots and cover with discs of waxed paper and cellophane.

We used a French yoghurt pot but any small glass jar would do. There won't be much room for decoration. We added a paper doily trimmed close to the rubber band, plus a small, plain self-adhesive label.

Apple and rosemary jelly

This is a variation on the lemon-thyme jelly theme, but as well as going with game and roast meats, it tastes good on toast. To make, adapt the recipe above and use half water to fruit.

Pot this jelly in slightly larger containers. We used a smallish, ordinary jam jar, and played up the delicate pink of the apple-jelly. We cut a top from an old pale pink muslin dress, but any circle of pinkish flimsy cotton would do. And we used pinking shears for an instantly pretty edge. Our label was a plain, self-adhesive white one, but we cut out a miniature picture of apple blossom, and added it on with a dab of Gloy. Sticking on cut-out pictures matches labels to ingredients.

Redcurrant jelly

This jelly is delectable eaten with roast lamb, but as redcurrants are never as plentiful as apples, we suggest making a small amount and potting it in really tiny pots, so each one is just enough for a single meal. Make the jelly like the basic apple jelly, simply scaling down the quantities.

We potted our jelly in the smallest glass pots possible, cutting down the waxed discs and cellophane tops to fit. As a stick-on label would have hidden most of the contents, we used a small, plain white tie-on label, and drew a fine red line around its edge. You'll find felt-tipped pens ideal for this purpose—they give really firm, dense lines of colour. We tied the label with cord.

19 Pork rillettes

Rillettes are fairly standard eating in France, but here you only find them in expensive restaurants. The ingredients are gratifyingly cheap.

Ingredients

450 g (1 lb) of belly of pork.
25 g (1 oz) of good lard.
13 g ($\frac{1}{2}$ oz) of salt.
Black pepper.
Spices to taste—nutmeg, mace etc.

Method

Cut the pork into small pieces and cook in the lard until very slightly coloured. Pour off the fat and keep it to one side. Continue cooking the pork up to 4 hours on a very low heat until soft and melting, adding a little water now and again.

The pork must not be allowed to dry out or harden. Let the pork cool and blend it very briefly in a liquidiser or processor. Add the salt, pepper and spices to taste, and pour on some of the fat you set aside. Pack the rillettes into small bowls, and pour at least half an inch of fat over the surface.

Although not shown in the photograph, we used a bowl that originally held supermarket paté, but any un-cracked earthenware or china bowls, or even mugs, are suitable. Decorate the top of the rillettes with a bay leaf and a peppercorn or two, or a sprig of fresh herbs in summer. Then pull Cling film tightly across the top, and tape it securely to the base with sellotape. If the rillettes are intended as a gift, tie on a plain label, explaining their contents and giving their shelf life.

20 Spiced plum jam

The cinnamon lifts this jam out of the ordinary, and if at the last minute you add some chopped almonds or walnuts, plus some fruit liqueur or brandy, it will turn into something extra special.

Ingredients

2.3 kg (5 lb) of red plums.
600 ml (1 pint) of water.
An 8 cm (3 in) stick of cinnamon.
2.3 kg (5 lb) of sugar.

Method

Simmer the plums and cinnamon in water until soft and pulpy. Remove stones as they float to the top. Stir in warmed sugar, and once dissolved, boil until a set is reached. Remove the cinnamon, and cool, pot and cover.

We used a French jam jar brought back from a holiday trip, but you can buy similar empty jars from branches of Habitat. The chic top is just a circle cut from a paper table napkin. This one's a stylish Marimekko design from Paperchase. The red and white, plus a red-edged label, emphasises the colour of the jam.

21 Dried fruit chutney

This piquant chutney makes all the difference to curries, cheeses and cold ham. And you could vary the spices.

Ingredients

900 g (2 lb) of dried mixed fruit, soaked overnight.
2 onions, chopped.
2 cloves of garlic, chopped small.
75 g of seedless raisins.
1 large cooking apple, peeled, cored and chopped.
450 g (1 lb) of sugar.
1 teaspoonful of ground turmeric.
25 g (1 oz) of whole pickling spice.
13 g ($\frac{1}{2}$ oz) of coriander seed.
5 ml (1 teaspoonful) of salt.
300 ml ($\frac{1}{2}$ pint) of malt vinegar.

Method

Cut the fruit into small pieces, removing any prune stones. Put in a saucepan with the onion, garlic, raisins, apple, turmeric, sugar and vinegar. Tie the spices and coriander seeds in a piece of muslin and add to the pan. Bring to the boil and simmer gently, with the lid on, for about an hour, stirring to prevent sticking. Remove the lid and continue cooking till the mixture is thick and jammy. Remove the spices and pot the chutney. Seal with Porosan to prevent evaporation.

22 Garlic and chilli vinegar

Use the vinegar for salad dressings, or add just a dash to mayonnaise, stews, spicy and fish dishes.

Ingredients

600 ml (1 pint) of wine or cider vinegar.
10 cloves of garlic.
4 fresh red and green chillies, halved and seeded.

Method

Bring the wine or vinegar to the boil and pour over the garlic and the chillies. Leave for six weeks; then bottle.

Use any glass bottle with a vinegar-proof top, if wide enough to take the chillies. We used a flagon; then tied on a hat of greaseproof paper with string.

23

A sailor's fancy piece

**If you can do a knot, you can do macramé.
It's satisfying, almost therapeutic
work that used to keep sailors
happy at sea. They'd have loved this
wall-hung stowaway.**

As soon as people discovered weaving, it was inevitable they'd discover macramé too. When they'd finished making a piece of cloth they had to do something to prevent the ends unravelling, and although they may have begun with simple knots, they'd soon have progressed to more decorative versions. An Assyrian frieze in the British Museum, dating from the 9th century BC, shows a warrior whose tunic is elaborately trimmed with a heavy fringe of macramé tassels.

The Moors are believed to have brought the art of macramé to Spain from its home in the Middle East. It then spread like wildfire throughout Europe, and when William of Orange's wife brought it from Holland to England, it became a fashionable pastime in court circles.

But it didn't stay an exclusive pursuit for long. Since macramé demands nothing but string and nimble fingers, it soon became popular with English sailors. Sailing ships in the 18th and 19th century needed men who were skilled at splicing and plaiting, and after working with thick ropes, working in string came easily.

Sometimes the sailors made presents for their wives. Sometimes they made mats, bags and sea-chest covers that they used to barter at ports of call. But most of all, they made string and canvas stowaways not dissimilar to the one we show in our photograph.

Hung alongside their hammocks—or their bunks if they were lucky—they provided handy storage for personal possessions without taking up floor space in their notoriously cramped quarters. They're ideal for the same reason in today's small bedrooms, particularly if bunk beds are being used, because there's an upper and a lower level pocket.

If you've never tackled macramé before, and would like to acquire some theoretical knowledge before embarking on our stowaway, page 122 suggests suitable reading. But you should be able to master the technique fairly easily, especially if you practise with ordinary string—you can always improvise a holding cord by tying the ends to the knobs of a drawer. We recommend smooth cotton twine for the actual work, because it allows the pattern of the knots to show more precisely. And if you really intend to take up macramé seriously, some craft shops sell special knotting boards, and special pins with T-shaped heads to prevent the twine slipping off.

Materials

Five 90-m spools of thick Cotton Seine Twine by Atlas Handicrafts (direct or mail order from Fred Aldous Crafts).

1.25 m of 130 cm (52 in) wide natural hessian (direct or mail order from The Felt & Hessian Shop).

A double long darning needle.

Method

To make pockets

Setting on: Cut a holding cord 60 cm (2 ft) long and secure to a knotting board as shown in Diagram 1. Cut 14 pieces of twine 45 cm (18 in) long; these will be used as leaders for the rows of horizontal cording. Cut 54 pieces of twine 2.8 m (8 ft 9 in) long, double them and set on to the holding cord as shown in Diagram 2.

The pattern: Each row of horizontal cording is worked with a separate leader as shown in Diagram 3. This is attached to the right side of the work. When the row has been worked, from right to left, which is easiest, the end of the leader is left pinned out of the way on the left side of the board, and all ends are sewn into the back of the work when it is finished.

*Step 1 With attached leader, work 2 rows of horizontal cording by making a double Half Hitch with each thread, as shown in Diagram 3.

Step 2 Divide threads into groups of 4, work 2 flat knots on each (Diagram 4). Repeat step 1.

Step 3 Divide threads into groups of 12. Work a double diagonal cross on each group as shown in Diagram 5 **. Repeat from * to ** twice more. Repeat step 1.

Leave an 8 cm (3 in) length of thread, trim across, unravel ends to form a fringe. Sew in ends of holding cord and attached leaders.

Work another pocket just the same.

To work the top fringe

Start by making the two loops, which are then incorporated into the fringe. For one loop:

* Cut 2 lengths 75 cm (2 ft 6 in), and 2 more 120 cm (4 ft) long.

Lay them together with ends level at the top, measure 30 cm (1 ft) from the top, make an overhand knot there over all 4 threads.

Pin knot to board.

Using the 2 shorter lengths as core threads, and the longer lengths each side as knotting threads, work 16 flat knots (Diagrams 4, 5 and 6).

Take off board, undo overhand knot **.

Repeat from * to ** once to make the other loop.

The fringe: This can be set on and worked in sections, as it is 49 cm (19½ in) long. Start from the right, and after the set-on threads reach the left side of the board, attach the leader and start working the pattern. When this is complete, move the work along and set on the next section.

Setting on: Cut a holding cord 60 cm (2 ft) long, and 4 more pieces of twine the same length to act as leaders for the horizontal cording. Cut 52 pieces of twine 60 cm (2 ft) long. Double 6 of these and set them on to the right side of the holding cord. Double one of the loops you have made, pin to board so that the flat knots finish level with the holding cord and, using the holding cord as leader, cord across with double Half Hitches all 8 threads to the left (Diagram 6). Double 40 of the 60 cm (2 ft) lengths and set on to the holding cord. Double the other loop and cord across as with the first loop, using the holding cord as leader. Double 6 of the 60 cm (2 ft) lengths and set on to the holding cord.

The pattern: Repeat step 1, as in bunk pocket pattern.

Repeat step 2, then repeat step 1 again.

Trim threads 5 cm (2 in) below last row of horizontal cording, unravel to form a fringe. Sew in ends of holding cord and attached leaders.

To make up the stowaway: Fold the hessian so that the selvedge comes at the bottom, and it measures 51 cm (20½ in) across. Seam along the top and side, taking a 1 cm (½ in) turning. Turn the right way out and press. Stitch the selvedge edges together along the bottom, on the right side. Place the top

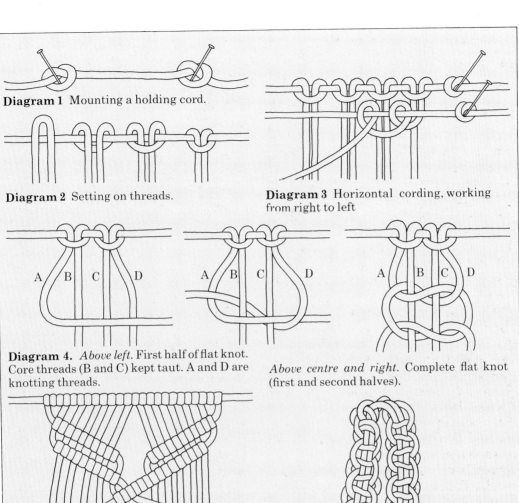

Diagram 1 Mounting a holding cord.

Diagram 2 Setting on threads.

Diagram 3 Horizontal cording, working from right to left

Diagram 4. *Above left*. First half of flat knot. Core threads (B and C) kept taut. A and D are knotting threads.

Above centre and right. Complete flat knot (first and second halves).

Diagram 5 Double diagonal cording, using outside thread as leader. Hold the leader at 45°. The leader of the first row is included in the knotting threads in the second row of the cording.

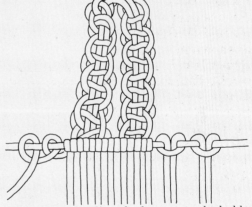

Diagram 6 Cording the loop on to the holding thread with a succession of double half-hitches.

fringe in position, and sew across the top over the holding cord, in between each set-on thread. All the sewing is done with the large darning needle, using a single strand of the unravelled twine. The twine unwinds into three strands. Sew across the top again, this time in between the two rows of horizontal cording at the lower edge.

Place the upper pocket in position 16 cm (6¼ in) from the top and 4 cm (1½ in) from each side. (As macramé work can be a little irregular, these measurements are approximate. Indeed, one of the charms of a natural craft like this is that minor discrepancies only add character). Sew down the sides with a strand of twine, and then stab stitch across the bottom between the two rows of horizontal cording. Position the lower pocket about 16 cm (6¼ in) below the lowest line of horizontal cording on the upper pocket, and sew on in the same way.

24

A crunchy crocheted collage of flowers

All crochet offers density and texture, but this tight-packed spray of jostled flowers creates an effect so three-dimensional, you could almost lift it out of the picture.

Crochet developed as an imitation of lace and originally sought to be fine and delicate. But even now, when it's become a technique in its own right, it is still mainly used to make flat "lacy" things like babies' shawls and tablecloths. That's why this flower picture is such a joy. It exploits the potential of crochet to the full, capitalising on its ability to look dense and textured and stand out boldly in rich relief.

One reason the flowers look so thick and natural is that they're worked in double knitting wool. This immediately gives them spring and body. Another is that they're only mounted by their centres, leaving the petals free to curl so the blooms look as if they're in the process of opening.

Although we suggest you use odd scraps of wool, it would be a pity to diverge from the colour scheme. The use of several shades of single colours infers the flowers and leaves are at different stages of development, just as they would be in a real bouquet.

If you're a beginner, you'll need to read a book about crochet, to become acquainted with the different stitches. (See page 126 for some suggestions.) But after just a little practice, this collage will be well within your scope. You'll soon find one of its chief advantages is that even if you've only got a few minutes, they'll be enough to work an individual flower. You can pick it up and put it down just as you fancy.

Materials

Oddments of double knitting wool in the following colours:

For the flowers, white, off-white, cream, pale gold, gold, pale yellow, deep yellow, orange, coral, bright burgundy, deep burgundy and dark brown.

For the leaves and stems, pale green, pale lime, mid-green, sea-green, dark green, beige, pale brown, mid-brown and dark brown.

A 3 mm (number 10) crochet hook.

A picture frame with inner measurements of about 33 cm (13 in) by 43 cm (17 in).

A piece of cardboard to fit the frame.

A piece of black felt to fit the cardboard.

A tube of Uhu glue.

Method

The following abbreviations are used throughout the instructions:

Ch. = chain; sl. st. = slip stitch; s.c. = single crochet; d.c. = double crochet; h. tr. = half treble; tr. = treble; d. tr. = double treble.

Start with the daisies: These are white with gold centres. Make two large daisies and four small daisies.

Round 1 With gold wool ch. 3 (rather loosely) and close into a ring with sl. st.

Round 2 Ch. 1 (to stand for 1 d.c.), and work 11 d.c. into ring (for small

daisies work 9 d.c.). Close with sl. st. (12 d.c.). Fasten off.

Round 3 Join white wool. Sl. st. to a d.c. of previous round. Ch. 7, 1 d.c. into same st. * ch. 7, 1 d.c. into next st., ch. 7, 1 d.c. into same st. * Repeat from * to * all round (24 petals). Fasten off.

Follow on with asters: Use variegated wools for the petals and dark brown for the centres. Make one large aster and two small asters.

Large: Round 1 With dark brown wool, ch. 4 (loosely). Close into a ring with sl. st.

Round 2 Ch. 2 (to stand for 1 tr.) and work 15 tr. into ring. Close with a sl. st. Fasten off.

Round 3 With variegated wool. Insert hook into a tr. of previous round * ch. 12, 1 d.c. into next tr. * (16 petals.) Repeat from * to * all round.

Round 4 As Round 3, but ch. 8 instead of 12, thus making a second row of smaller petals in front of the first.

Small: Worked as above with following amendments:

Round 1 Ch. 3.

Round 2 Ch. 2 work 12 h. tr. into ring.

Round 3 Ch. 9 instead of 12.

Round 4 Ch. 6 instead of 8.

Make the spray of blossom: Work three lengths of blossom—two in off-white wool and one in white wool. Ch. 5. Join with sl. st. to first ch. (bud). Ch. 4 (for stem), * ch. 5, sl. st. to first of 5 ch. * Repeat from * to * 3 times more then sl. st. to first ch. of the group (4-petalled flower). Ch. 3 or 4 and make another flower. Repeat until there are 4 or 5 flowers along the chain stem.

Crochet all the primulas: These are made in exactly the same way as the blossom, but with five petals to a flower. Start by * ch. 5, sl. st. to first of 5 ch. * Repeat from * to * 4 times and sl. st. to first ch. of the group. Work only 2 or 3 ch. between each flower so that these "stems" are hidden when the flowers are massed.

Make 13 clusters of flowers as follows, which are finally arranged as four groups:

1. 3 pale yellow, 3 cream, 3 deep yellow, 2 gold (4 clusters).
2. As above but with 3 gold instead of 2 (4 clusters).
3. 2 orange, 2 gold, 2 pale gold (3 clusters).
4. 3 deep burgundy, 3 bright burgundy (2 clusters).

Continue with the primula leaves: Make three in dark green and three in sea-green. Ch. 8. Inserting hook first into 4th ch. from hook, work along chain as follows: 2 tr., 1 d. tr., 2 d. tr. in next ch., 7 d. tr. in last ch. (to turn for point). Work back along the other side of chain reversing stitch order, ie 2 d. tr. into next ch., 1 d. tr., 2 tr., sl. st. into last ch. Fasten off.

Make the bell flowers: Make two groups—one of three off-white flowers with pale green cups; and one of five flowers, two in pale green with darker green cups and three in pale lime with paler green cups. Start with green wool for the cups or calyx.

Round 1 Ch. 3 and close into a ring with sl. st.

Round 2 Ch. 2 (to stand for 1 tr.) and work 9 tr. into ring. Close with sl. st. (10 tr.).

Round 3 Work 2 ch., 1 d.c. into first tr. Miss one st. Repeat all round (5 loops).

Round 4 In each of the 5 loops of previous round work 1 d.c., 1 h. tr., 1 tr., 1 h. tr., 1 d.c.

Round 5 Join new colour for flower bell. Turn work so that inside of work is facing you. Sl. st. into space between last d.c. of one petal and first d.c. of next, ch. 3, 1 d.c. into space between next two petals. Repeat (5 loops).

Round 6 As Round 4. Fasten off.

Create the roses: Make one each in coral, orange, deep yellow, pale yellow and cream.

Round 1 Ch. 4 and join into a loop with sl. st. Into loop work 1 d.c. into first ch. * ch. 7, 1 d.c. into next ch * repeat from * to * twice more ending with ch. 7, 1 sl. st. into first d.c. (4 loops made).

Round 2 Join new colour. 1 d.c. into same place as last sl. st. * 5 tr. into next loop 1 d.c. into next d.c. * repeat from * to * twice more ending with 5 tr. into last loop 1 sl. st. into first d.c.

Round 3 1 d.c. into same place as last sl. st. * ch. 3 miss 4 sts. 1 d.c. into next st. * repeat from * to * 3 times more. For last loop work ch. 3 miss 3 sts. 1 sl. st. into first d.c. (5 loops).

Round 4 1 d.c. into same place as last sl. st. * 3 d.c. into next loop 1 d.c. into d.c. between loops. * Repeat from * to * 3 times, ending with 3 d.c. into last loop 1 sl. st. into first d.c.

Round 5 Join new colour. 1 s.c. into same place as last sl. st. then over each petal work as follows: 1 d.c., 2 tr. into first d.c., 3 d. tr. into second d.c., 2 tr., 1 d.c. into third d.c. with 1 s.c. into the d.c. between each petal. At end omit 1 s.c. and sl. st. into first s.c.

Round 6 1 d.c. into same place as last sl. st. * ch. 3 miss 6 sts. 1 d.c. into next st. * repeat from * to * 5 times more. For last loop work ch. 3 miss 7 sts. 1 sl. st. into first d.c. (7 loops).

Round 7 Same as Round 4 except repeat from * to * 5 times more.

Round 8 Join new colour. Work as for Round 5.

Round 9 1 d.c. into same place as last sl. st. *. Ch. 3 miss 7 sts. 1 d.c. into next st. * repeat from * to * 6 times more, then ch. 3 miss 6 sts. 1 d.c. into next st. ch. 3 miss 6 sts. 1 sl. st. into first d.c. (9 loops).

Round 10 Same as Round 4 except repeat from * to * 7 times more.

Round 11 Join new colour. Work as for Round 5.

Add the rosebuds: Make three in varying shades from cream to coral. Ch. 12. Into 4th ch. from hook work 1 tr., 3 tr. into same space, * 5 tr. into next ch. Repeat from * to end. Fasten off. Use 3 shades of wool for each rosebud, working a few trebles in each. Make 2 this size and 1 smaller by chaining 9 to start.

Crochet the large rose leaves: Ch. 12. Inserting hook first into 4th ch. from hook work along chain as follows: 2 tr., 2 d. tr., 1 tr., 1 h. tr., 1 d.c., 3 s.c. into last ch. (to turn for point). Work back along other side of ch. reversing stitch order, ie 1 d.c., 1 h. tr., 1 tr., 2 d. tr., 2 tr., sl. st. to last ch. Ch. 3 for stalk. Fasten off.

Now make the small leaves: These are made as above, but ch. 11 to start and omit one of the d. tr. on each side of the leaf.

These leaves are made separately and sewn to stems of 30 ch. to form 4 sprays, thus:

1. 5 large brown leaves (a rosebud is sewn to this spray).

2. 4 pale brown leaves (small).

3. 2 large and 3 small leaves in shades of green (2 rosebuds are sewn to this).

4. 3 small green leaves.

Finish with the stems: Make the stems of 30 ch. as follows:

Two in green for the bell flowers.

One in pale brown, one in brown, two in green for the rose leaf sprays.

Two in beige, three in brown and three in dark brown for the stems of the bouquet.

To make up the collage: Thread in all the ends neatly. Do *not* press the work. Sew the bell flowers to the stems and make up the rose leaf sprays as previously indicated. Group the flowers on the felt as shown in the photograph, arranging the leaf sprays and stems first. Surplus stems are hidden by large flower heads.

Then mark the positions with French chalk and/or pins, remove, and glue with Uhu. Only glue the centres of flowers and the bases of leaves, so the petals and leaves can curl naturally. When dry, glue the felt to the cardboard, and mount in a frame. Old walnut or another wood is very nice.

25

A little gentle stencilling

Most stencils get painted with a brush, but the colour was finely sprayed onto these stencilled cushions to give softer and much more sensitive results.

Although we could have sprayed these stencils with Holts Dupli-Color car sprays, which come in easy to operate aerosols, the cushion covers would then have needed careful hand washing. Since we preferred the idea of dropping them in the washing machine, we used washable fabric paints that came in pots, and needed blowing through a pipette.

It's true this was a fairly lengthy procedure, and you might prefer to use the same washable paints, but simply brush them on instead. If you do, however, you'll lose the capacity to overlap the colours gradually, so delicate shades merge imperceptibly. Using the more tricky spray technique, you can add the bloom to a grape or the blush to a rose with a mastery artists like Jan van Huysen would have envied.

We cut the stencils to our own design, and you could easily do the same. Alternatively, most big stationers sell ready-cut designs. Lyn le Grice's Country Collection stencils (from Paperchase direct or mail order) are undoubtedly the most beautiful available, but they're really meant for making great sweeping swags and borders. You could, however, just use a section. Paperchase also sell a range of stencil books with different designs on every page—you pull out the pages, soak them in linseed oil for an impervious-to-paint surface, cut out the

designs—and there are your stencils. As the scale of design is dictated by the pages, you may need to build it up for large sized cushions by adding one of the many attractive borders also included in the book.

It's possible to stencil any plain, flat surface, from walls to floors to items of furniture. (Holts' car sprays are best suited to these situations—but read directions for required safety precautions.) In past centuries stencils were used mainly on walls because wallpaper was extremely expensive. The early settlers in America employed the technique widely because imported papers were even more prohibitively priced. This explains why the range of Paperchase stencil books includes titles like Early American and Pennsylvanian Dutch.

But although it was also used on furniture, it was seldom used on floors as it is today. There's enormous scope for decorating plain floorboards. You can confine yourself to just a border round the edges, where the stencils would get little wear and tear. Or you could scatter the floor with "Persian rugs", creating a virtual trompe l'oeil effect. In either case, it would be advisable to add three or four protective coats of clear Polyurethane varnish to provide a practical finish.

The only risk with stencilling lies in overdoing it. Too little is always better than too much. So exploit what's really its main advantage—the ability to apply pattern solely where pattern is needed—perhaps on the wooden risers of a characterless staircase, or to form borders round windows that need more importance. And appreciate it's flexible colour potential. Instead of searching endlessly for wallpapers or curtains to go with your existing furnishings, you can simply pick the precise shades you need.

Our cushion covers are sophisticated examples of stencilling. Because we wanted to use several colours, we had to mask out previous colours every time we sprayed on new ones. But don't feel obliged to be so ambitious. Since stencilling never turns out the same way twice (the density and texture of the paint always vary) you could still get highly individual results by sticking to a single colour. There'd be no danger of your cushions looking mass-produced; each one would have its own special character.

Materials

Ready cut stencils or Stencil paper.
A craft knife.
Some sheets of thick paper to use as masks.
Some masking tape (all from good craft and art shops).
A drawing board or an old wooden pastry board.
Medium-weight calico (from John Lewis and John Lewis Partnership branches).
A spray diffuser (from Cowling & Wilcox or local craft or art shops).
1 pot of Chestnut F4 Dylon Color-Fun fabric paint.
1 pot of London Red F6 Dylon Colour-Fun fabric paint.
1 pot of Texan Gold F2 Dylon Colour-Fun fabric paint.
1 pot of Fiji Blue F9 Dylon Colour-Fun fabric paint (all from most department stores).

Method

To cut your own stencil: Trace the design onto tracing paper. It will need a strong and immediately recognisable outline, like a pair of birds, a weeping willow or a bowl of flowers. You could, of course, copy our designs. To provide the design with detail within the outline, draw in "bridges" (ie thin strips that separate the different elements). In our basket of roses cushion covers, for instance, these show as the lines of unpainted calico between the petals of the roses, between the leaves, and between the weave of the basket. Be sure the bridges follow the natural contours of the design, and always make them at least 0.2 mm ($\frac{1}{8}$ in) thick.

Cut the stencil paper slightly larger than the design, leaving at least 2.5 cm (1 in) all around. Pin it to the wooden drawing board or pastry board. Place some carbon paper on the stencil paper, and retrace the design from the tracing paper onto the stencil paper. Cut the design with a craft knife, holding it almost perpendicular, but leaning slightly outwards to give a bevelled edge. It may help to think of the design in terms of a photographic negative. The areas you cut out will be the areas that get painted; the areas you don't cut will stay as plain calico.

General preparation: Wash the calico to get rid of the dressing. Otherwise the fabric paint will lie on the surface and may disappear at the first wash. Press the calico, and cut it to the size required for your cushions.

Lay it on a firm wooden surface like an old table, drawing board or pastry board. Pin the stencil on the fabric with drawing pins or dressmaking pins, taking care to secure it along the bridges within the design as well as round the edges. This will prevent any paint creeping behind the stencil onto areas that are meant to be left unpainted. (If you were stencilling a hard surface instead of fabric, you could stick down the bridges with Bostik Blu-Tack and use masking tape to secure the edges.)

Finally, cover the surrounding work area with plenty of newspapers or an old sheet—it's impossible to confine sprayed paint to a designated area.

Learning the spray technique: Dilute the fabric paints up to 50% with water in something like clean yoghurt containers. If you dilute the paint more, the colour will get weak and tend to "spread". Although the paints are intermixable, do not premix them in the pots, or you will lose the speckled, grainy look that is the whole point of spraying instead of brush-painting with brushes.

Now practise the art of spraying—first on paper until you're fairly confident, then on an offcut of calico to gauge the true effect. Put the diffuser's fine tube into a container of diluted paint, blow through the fatter tube, and the colour will spray through the top of the fine tube. (If it doesn't, you need to blow *harder*.)

The main things to learn during the rehearsal stage are how to apply the paint lightly and finely—it's important to underspray rather than overspray, because you can always add more paint but you can't subtract—and how to overlap the basic colours with subtlety. Practise spraying Fiji Blue finely over Texan Gold to make green; Fiji Blue over a light base of London Red to make purple; London Red sparingly over Texan Gold to make orange. To maintain the clarity of colour, it's absolutely essential to wash the diffuser out between each and every application of paint.

To stencil the cushion covers: Leaving only the basket area of the design exposed, mask out all the rest of the stencil with thick paper stuck on with masking tape, and spray the basket lightly with Chestnut. If you want to deepen the colour, wait for the paint to dry before applying another fine coat and repeat as often as necessary. When you are sure the paint has finally dried, remove the mask, and cut another from thick paper to cover the basket and all the rest of the design except the next area you intend to spray—perhaps an individual fruit or flower. Always waiting for the paint to dry between different applications, continue masking and spraying until the entire design is painted.

We decided to quilt two of our cushion covers before making them up, to establish a rather 18th-century mood, but this isn't necessary—it's very much an optional extra.

26

The cat sat on the mat

Although this tapestry features a tabby, you could easily have your own cat in stitches. Just adapt the colour and markings to match the characteristics of your particular puss.

The marvellous thing about needle-point (or tapestry as most of us call it), is that it's as easy as painting by numbers. You simply can't go wrong if you follow the pattern, and a beginner can produce really expert results that will win admiration from the un-initiated. This tapestry, in basic tent stitch, is even easier than most.

Materials

A piece of single-thread tapestry canvas measuring 30 cm (12 in) by 45 cm (18 in) with 13 holes to the inch. (As this comes 90 cm (36 in) wide, you've no choice but to buy twice as much as you need—but if you catch the tapestry bug, it will come in useful).

Anchor tapisserie wools: two each of 067, 0366, 0498, 0848 and 0894; one each of 013, 019, 0170, 0315, 0386, 0392, 0984, 0986 and 0987.

A packet of Milwards size 18–24 tapestry needles (these are not sold individually).

A packet of whiskers.

A small brass bell.

Some strong thread. (All available from specialist needlework shops, and the art-needlework departments of most big stores.)

A picture frame (if possible, from a junk shop or jumble sale—it doesn't matter if the glass is broken because you won't need it).

A small, hand-held tapestry frame (from specialist needlework shops and art-needlework departments).

NB If your picture frame is made of softwood and not too deep (in which case there wouldn't be enough canvas to carry round to the back), you could use it as a tapestry frame by pulling the canvas straight and taut, tugging it over the edges of the frame, and fixing on the back with drawing pins.

Method

Mark the centre of the canvas each way with a line of tacking stitches. Although the actual tapestry only measures about 19 cm ($7\frac{1}{2}$ in) by 25 cm (10 in), while your piece of cut canvas measures 30 cm (12 in) by 45 cm (18 in), you will need the blank border when you come to frame the finished result. To prevent the raw edges fraying as you work, turn them in by 1 cm ($\frac{1}{2}$ in), press in position, and tack all around.

Mount the canvas over whichever kind of frame you are using (ie with drawing pins at 5 cm (2 in) intervals for the picture frame; if you are using a commercial frame, ask the retailer to explain the mounting procedure, as this varies).

Now look at the pattern printed over the page. Each square represents a single stitch, so that if you follow it precisely, you will be sure of success. The arrows at the left and below the pattern indicate the centres, and must, of course, correspond to

your tacking stitches. The key of symbols above the pattern represents the colours you should use; you can either follow these literally, or adapt them if you are portraying your own cat.

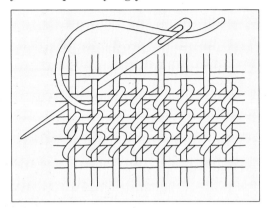

Some tips for beginners: As you can see from the diagram just above, tent stitch (or petit point) really is easy. It consists of slanting the wool from left to right over one crossing of the canvas threads, and then slanting it from right to left (as shown) under two crossings. For return rows, turn the tapestry upside down and repeat.

If you do make a stitch wrongly, and only discover it when you're too far past to face unpicking your work, you can usually correct it by adding another stitch on top. Unless you're a perfectionist, mistakes aren't worth agonising over.

Be careful about the following, however. Never make knots. Leave loose ends on the back, and oversew them in the normal course of your stitching. Never thread your needle with more than 50 cm (19½ in) of wool—if you do, it will wear thin and finally break. And allow the wool to untwist itself every so often for even texture.

Starting the actual stitching: Theoretically, you should start stitching from the centre of the pattern, marked at the point where your lines of tacking cross over. But if you can't resist beginning with the cat's face (commencing at the eyes and then filling out), there's no real reason why

you shouldn't do so.

Squaring up the results: Having done all the stitching, it's just possible that when you take your completed canvas off the working frame, you'll find it has been pulled out of shape, giving the cat a lopsided look. If this has happened, you must straighten it before finally framing it. The best way is to pin a piece of graph paper to a drawing board or pastry board, place the canvas face down onto it and, working one side at a time, secure the canvas with drawing pins at 2.5 cm (1 in) intervals, lining it up with the lines of the graph paper. The first two sides should be relatively easy, but you'll probably have difficulty stretching the last two into position. If so, damp the back of the tapestry with water to make it more pliable. Once all square and ship-shape, leave for 24 hours to dry out, before unpinning.

Putting on the style: Now it's time for the whiskers and the bell. Thread one of the whiskers through an ordinary sewing needle and make a small securing back-stitch on the reverse of the canvas where you want the whisker to "grow"; then pass the needle through to the right side of the canvas and release the whisker.

Continue with the rest of the whiskers, and if you'd like them to curl, wrap them round a pencil, pulling tight as you release them, continuing until you're happy with the result. Trim the whiskers if required. As for the bell, working from the back of the canvas, simply fix it in the centre of the collar with a single stitch.

Finally, place the tapestry centrally over the backing board of your picture frame, and secure down one side by pinning it into the edges of the board with drawing pins. Repeat down the other three sides, tugging to make sure the tapestry is taut. Then, using a needle and strong thread, lace from side to side in both directions. Remove pins, and frame the tapestry.

Key to diagram
Tapisserie wool

◙ - 067   ⊡ - 0386   T - 0894
◪ - 0170   ☑ - 0392   ◙ - 0984
◙ - 013   ⊙ - 0315   ☐ - 0498   ☒ - 0986
◙ - 019   ☑ - 0366   ◙ - 0848   ◤ - 0987

—67—

27

A pocket handkerchief patchwork

**This patchwork quilt is almost instant.
You could run it up on a machine
in one industrious evening—or take
your time, and spread the work
throughout the week.**

Familiarity breeds contempt. Whoever really looks at men's coloured handkerchiefs—the ordinary, traditional kind—that get used, washed and hurriedly ironed? Yet they're beautifully and graphically designed, with fine precise borders and careful colour combinations. In fact, they're almost minor works of art, and when they're sewn together into a bold-squared patchwork and criss-crossed diagonally with quilting stitches, the result, as you can see for yourself, is extraordinarily chic and sophisticated.

Materials

30 men's handkerchiefs, each about 40 cm (16 in) square, but allow 36 handkerchiefs for a larger-size double quilt.

An old, double-size, wincyette sheet for the interlining.

A double-size cotton sheet in a related colour for the backing; or sheeting by the metre (from Limericks, mail order only).

NB If you want a warmer quilt (this one's strictly summer-weight), consider buying terylene wadding by the metre for the interlining (from John Lewis and John Lewis Partnership stores).

Method

Spread all the handkerchiefs on the floor, and arrange so the different colour-tones balance. It may help to screw your eyes up as you look at them; this way the strongest-coloured hankies "jump out", and you can then make a point of distributing them fairly evenly.

Once you're happy with the arrangement, machine the handkerchiefs together. You'll find it easiest if you work in strips from top to bottom, and then sew the strips together.

Now make a "sandwich" of the three layers of your quilt. Lay your backing fabric, which needs to be at least 10 cm (4 in) larger all round than your quilt-top, wrong side up. (If you've made it from by-the-metre sheeting, iron any seams open.) Then lay the interlining, which needs to be the same size as the quilt-top, on top—making sure the same amount of backing fabric shows all round. Finally, lay the handkerchief quilt-top on the interlining, right side up, smooth the three layers flat, pin them together and tack securely.

To stitch the quilting: Using tailor's chalk and a long ruler, draw diagonal lines across the quilt in both directions, so that they pass through the corners of individual handkerchiefs to intersect at their centres. *NB* Do not draw the lines from corner to corner of the quilt, unless you happen to be making a square quilt, or they will fail to pass through the handkerchief corners.

Machine over the tailor's chalk, stitching the longest diagonals first,

and working from top right to bottom left; then bottom right to top left. When you've finished machining, brush off the tailor's chalk, and undo the tacking stitches.

Finally, cut away the surplus interlining, and fold the backing fabric three times to make a border that overlaps the quilt-top. When machined in place, the border will provide a cleverly co-ordinated trim. It's this kind of last-minute attention to detail that can make the very nice look superlatively good.

28

A bouquet in a basket

**Pressed flower pictures look delicate—but
meagre and sparse. This picture
uses dried flowers instead, and the generous
result is full of vigour. It will always
be alive and thriving.**

Dried flowers are strong and three-dimensional. They retain their original overall form, and this is an extremely important factor. The beauty of any bloom lies, not just in itself, but in the way it springs from its supporting stem. If you can keep this movement, you keep the flowers "alive" even though their colour has long since faded.

This accounts for the success of our dried flower picture. Although it has a muted, non-colour theme, which has been deliberately played up with a suede brown background, the blooms still seem to be bursting with energy. They look as free and natural as if they've just been picked.

Unlike pressing flowers—which demands endless care, and then produces a flat and static result—drying flowers is a very simple process. And as you're using big sprays instead of individual blooms, it's much easier to amass material. Of course, as the finished picture will have plenty of depth, you will need a correspondingly deep box frame. A latch at back could be useful for repairs.

Materials

Hydrangeas.
Anaphalous (an easy-to-grow annual with clusters of little white flowers).
Golden rod.
A few well-shaped sprays of ivy, beech, laurel and box.

Any attractive extras gleaned from the hedgerows.
Glycerine (from chemist shops).
1 can of off-white and 1 can of pale beige Holts' car spray (from car accessory shops), for spraying some of the hydrangeas. This is optional.
A small cane bowl or basket, from which a section can be cut.
A piece of stiff card for a mount.
A slightly larger piece of fabric, like imitation suede or velvet, for covering the mount.
A tube of Copydex adhesive.
A tube of Uhu glue.
A box frame with a depth of at least 5 cm (2 in).

Method

Both flowers and leaves should be picked on a fine day when they are dry. Always gather more than you think you'll need. Then you'll be sure of having suitable shapes for your arrangement, and you'll be covered in case of any failures.

Pick the golden rod and anaphalous just before the flowers come to maturity. And choose the hydrangeas with great care, as the gathering time is all-important. The true flower of the hydrangea is a small central swelling. What we think of as the colourful petals are really bracts or modified leaves. Pick the hydrangeas when the true flower is over and the bracts are no longer fleshy, but papery to the

touch and beginning to change colour. If you pick them too soon, the bracts will shrivel up.

Gather the foliage in late summer to early autumn. The leaves need to be mature, but they should not yet have started to take on autumnal tints.

To preserve the flowers: Strip the foliage from the stems of the golden rod and the anaphalous and tie the flowers in bundles, leaving a loop so that they can be hung upside down in a dry, airy and preferably dark place. Check the ties periodically, because the stems shrink while drying and some flowers could fall out. Leave them until both flowers and stems have become stiff, which should take about three weeks.

Arrange the hydrangeas loosely in a vase with a little water, and allow them to take it all up. Don't replace the water, but leave the hydrangeas to dry in the vase until they are crisp.

If you're going to spray them with car paint, wait until you're nearly ready to assemble the picture, so the colour stays fresh and dust free. And do choose a soft and subtle colour that will be sympathetic to the neutral shades elsewhere. As the fumes of car sprays can be harmful if inhaled, try to spray the hydrangeas out of doors, and if possible, wear a protective face mask. A Boots' smog mask would be both cheap and effective.

To preserve the leaves: These are preserved by an entirely different method from the flowers, which gives them a lustrous, slightly waxy look, and turns them mellow shades of brown. Prepare the leaf sprays by stripping off the lower leaves. Crush the stems at the bottom, and immerse them in water for an hour or two after gathering.

Mix together one part of glycerine to two parts of boiling water. Leave the mixture to cool, and pour it into tallish narrow containers (if you can spare any vases they'll do fine), to a depth of 10 cm (4 in) to 15 cm (6 in). Stand the foliage in the containers and leave until all the leaves in each individual spray have turned a uniform colour, and the leaves feel supple to the touch. This could take anything from a few days to three weeks or so. Remove the foliage and dry it gently with a soft cloth.

Deciding on the frame: If you're going to use an existing box frame, it's vital you find it at this stage. Junk and antique shops are a good source of Victorian versions, though you can sometimes strike lucky at a jumble sale. This is because the way you arrange the flowers is crucial to the success of the picture, and you'll need to fit the arrangement to the frame, not vice versa. If you're having a box frame specially made—in which case ask for a depth of at least 5 cm (2 in)—you're free, of course, to arrange the flowers in any shape and to any scale of mount you fancy. This might seem the ideal situation but oddly enough, in practice, it helps to have limits.

To make the mount: Cut the card to the size of the frame you have, or intend to have, to provide a mount. Cut the background fabric to the same size as the mount plus a 2.5 cm (1 in) allowance all around. Centre the card on the wrong side of the fabric and stick in place with Copydex, applying the adhesive round the edges only. Trim off the excess fabric.

To prepare the wicker basket: Make a "basket" by cutting off an appropriately sized section from a cane bowl or basket. In our 52 cm (20½ in) by 59 cm (23½ in) picture, the section of basket measured about 20 cm (8 in) at its widest and 10 cm (4 in) high. If you're taking the section from a circular bowl or basket, and find it's too rounded to fit within the depth of your frame, you can flatten it quite easily. Immerse it in cold water for a few minutes; then shape with the fingers and dry between sheets of newspaper with a weight on top. If the section threatens to unravel at the edges, fix the stray ends in place with Uhu glue. And if the cane is fairly open-weave, so the stems of the dried flowers are likely to show through it, line the inside of the basket with a scrap of appropriately coloured fabric.

To assemble the picture: Begin with a "dry run". Position the basket on the mount, and then arrange the flowers just as you would in a vase, with all the stems and sprays radiating from the centre of the basket. It's best to concentrate on getting the basic shape first, building it up with the beech leaves, ivy sprays and laurel leaves etc, and adding the flowers last. Check everything against the depth of the frame as you work; if anything projects too far it will get crushed against the glass, and the picture will lose the sense of freedom and movement that's the whole point of making an arrangement of this type.

Once you're satisfied with the arrangement, mark the major positions with French chalk and stick everything back into place with Uhu glue, again starting with the background foliage. Finally, check everything is securely glued by gently turning the picture upside down and shaking it. If anything's going to fall off, it's best it does it now, before it's trapped behind the glass of the frame.

Some advice on pressed flowers: Although we've been fairly dismissive of pressed flowers, they do have one overriding advantage—they're capable of retaining their colour. However, some are much more capable than others, and its worth knowing which to avoid disappointment.

Shades of violet are probably the easiest to preserve. Flowers like rosebay willow herb and violas always look well, but as soon as you start moving into the blues, the chances of success become more slender. It's often possible to keep the dark purple-blue of larkspur, but truly blue flowers like forget-me-nots will tend to fade to a dirty beige. Still they're worth trying —one or two may work. Yellows and oranges are usually reliable, but reds sometimes dry to a brownish colour, particularly the brilliant red of geranium. White flowers, even though they may turn creamy, will always produce attractive results.

Leaves tend to stay green with the exception of shiny ones, which dry to a dull and dreary beige. Silver foliage stays true, as does the majority of autumn-tinted foliage.

It's best to avoid succulents and fleshy-leafed plants because their high water content makes them difficult to dry. This rules out orchids and even African violets. But fibrous plants respond well to pressing. The anapholous we used in the dried flower picture would prove an ideal subject for pressing too, although of course, each tiny flower would need removing first. It's always necessary to press flower heads quite separately, removing them from their stems and leaves.

Some flowers, like lily of the valley, demand to be pressed in profile. But it's possible to press even a daffodil full face, provided you slit the trumpet into flexible petals.

Other flowers, like passion flowers, can be pressed full face, but only when the stamens and pistil have been removed to prevent them bruising the petals underneath. The stamens and pistils should be pressed separately for sticking back later.

There's no mystique about the actual pressing. Basically, all you need is to lay the flowers, untouching, between two sheets of blotting paper which have been inserted into a heavy book, and then pile more heavy books on top. Telephone directories are ideal for the job. This should give as good results as the commercial frames on sale in craft shops and most department stores. And it would be much cheaper.

29

A creamy Aran bedspread

This bedspread's a family heirloom of the future. We're not pretending it's cheap or speedy to make—but it will be an achievement to be proud of.

The Aran islands lie off the west coast of Ireland on the outer edge of Galway Bay. The island women are world-famous for the jerseys they knit in wonderful thick creamy-white pure wool, incorporating intricate patterns that are quite unique. These patterns are never written down but handed on in families through the generations.

We decided to steal six of the Aran patterns and use them as the basis of this bedspread. Knitted into what are virtually "sampler" squares, they're joined with wide strips of double moss stitch and cable, with a narrower but matching strip for the border. The result is so luxuriously heavy, it's stable enough to need no backing.

Since the bedspread is based on individual squares, we wish we could suggest you hand them out amongst the family, so everyone shares in this worthwhile project. But sadly, uniform tension is all-important. Without it, the squares will not marry up truly and the completed article will not lie flat. Each completed "sampler" should measure 23 cm (9 in) square.

Materials

For double bedspread, 204.5 cm (80½ in) wide by 273 cm (107½ in) long, you'll need:

About 102 fifty-gram balls of Marriner Choice Aran pure new wool (from R. V. Marriner).

1 pair 4 mm knitting needles—English

size 8.

1 pair 4½ mm knitting needles—English size 7.

1 pair 5 mm knitting needles—English size 6.

1 cable needle.

NB You'll need to make eight of each square for a double-bedspread.

For a single-bedspread, 158.5cm (62½in) wide by 273cm (107½in) long, you'll need:

About 77 fifty-gram balls of Marriner Choice Aran pure new wool.

The same needles as above.

NB You'll need to make six of each square for a single-bedspread.

Abbreviations: K, knit; p, purl; st(s), stitch(es); tog, together; patt, pattern; rep, repeat; inc, increasing; dec, decreasing; sl, slip; alt, alternate; Cr2F, cross 2 front by knitting into the front of the 2nd st on left hand needle then into first st and slipping both off needle; Cr2B, cross 2 back by knitting into back of 2nd st on left hand needle then into front of first st and slipping both off needle; Cr3F, cross 3 front by slipping next 2 sts onto cable needle, leave at front of work, p1, k2 from cable needle; Cr3B, cross 3 back by slipping next st onto cable needle, leave at back of work, k2, p st from cable needle; C2F, cable 2 front by slipping next 2 sts onto cable needle, leave at front of work, p2, k2 from cable needle; C2B, cable 2 back by slipping next 2 sts onto cable needle, leave at back of work, k2, p2 from cable needle; C3F, cable 3 front by slipping next 2 sts onto cable needle, leave at front of work, k1, k2 from cable needle; C4F, cable 4 front by slipping next 2 sts onto cable needle, leave at front, k2, k2 from cable needle; C4B, cable 4 back by slipping next 2 sts onto cable needle, leave at back, k2, k2 from cable needle.

Method

To make Square A:
Using size 5 mm needles, cast on 58 sts.

1st row: K1, p to last st, k1.

2nd row: K1, * (k1, p1, k1) all into next st, p3 tog, rep from * to last st, k1.

3rd row: As 1st row.

4th row: K1, * p3 tog, (k1, p1, k1) all into next st, rep from * to last st, k1.

These 4 rows form the pattern and are repeated. Continue in patt until work measures 23 cm (9 in), ending with a wrong side row. Cast off.

To make Square B:
Using size 4 mm needles, cast on 58 sts.

1st row: K1, p1, (k2, p2) twice, k16, p2, k2, p2, k16, (p2, k2) twice, p1, k1.

2nd and every alt row: K2, (p2, k2) twice, p16, k2, p2, k2, p16, (k2, p2) twice, k2.

3rd row: K1, p1, (Cr2F, p2) twice, k4, C4B, C4F, k4, p2, Cr2F, p2, k4, C4B, C4F, k4, (p2, Cr2F) twice, p1, k1.

5th row: K1, p1, (Cr2F, p2) twice, k2, C4B, k4, C4F, k2, p2, Cr2F, p2, k2, C4B, k4, C4F, k2, (p2, Cr2F) twice, p1, k1.

7th row: K1, p1, (Cr2F, p2) twice, C4B, k8, C4F, p2, Cr2F, p2, C4B, k8, C4F, (p2, Cr2F) twice, p1, k1.

8th row: K2, (p2, k2) twice, p16, k2, p2, k2, p16, (k2, p2) twice, k2.

The last 6 rows form the pattern and are repeated. Continue in patt until work measures 23 cm (9 in), ending with a wrong side row. Cast off.

To make Square C:
Using size 5 mm needles, cast on 56 sts.

1st row: K1, * k2, p4, rep from * to last st, k1.

2nd row: K1, * C4F, p2, rep from * to last st, k1.

3rd row: As 1st row.

4th row: K1, p2, * k2, C2B, rep from * to last 5 sts, k5.

5th row: K1, * p4, k2, rep from * to last st, k1.

6th row: K1, * p2, C4B, rep from * to last st, k1.

7th row: As 5th row.

8th row: K5, * C2F, k2, rep from * to last 3 sts, p2, k1.

These 8 rows form the pattern and are repeated. Continue in patt until work measures 23 cm (9 in), ending with a wrong side row. Cast off.

To make Square D:
Using size 4½ mm needles, cast on 56 sts.
1st row: K1, p20, k2, p4, k2, p4, k2, p20, k1.
2nd row: K1, (Cr2B, Cr2F) 5 times, p2, C4F, p2, C4B, p2, (Cr2B, Cr2F) 5 times, k1.
3rd row: K1, p20, (k2, p4) twice, k2, p20, k1.
4th row: K1, (Cr2F, Cr2B) 5 times, (p2, k4) twice, p2, (Cr2F, Cr2B) 5 times, k1.
5th row: As 2nd row.

The last 4 rows form the pattern and are repeated. Continue in patt until work measures 23 cm (9 in), ending with a wrong side row. Cast off.

To make Square E:
Using size 4½ mm needles, cast on 66 sts.
1st row: K.
2nd and every alt row: K1, p to last st, k1.
3rd row: K1, * C4B, C4F, rep from * to last st, k1.
5th row: K.
7th row: K1, * C4F, C4B, rep from * to last st, k1.
8th row: K1, p to last st, k1.

These 8 rows form the pattern and are repeated. Continue in patt until work measures 23 cm (9 in), ending with a 4th or 8th patt row. Cast off.

To make Square F:
Using size 4 mm needles, cast on 56 sts.
1st row: K4, * p4, C4F, p4, rep from * to last 4 sts, k4.
2nd row: (K1, p1) twice, * k4, p4, k4, rep from * to last 4 sts, (p1, k1) twice.
3rd row: K4, * p3, Cr3B, C3F, p3, rep from * to last 4 sts, k4.
4th row: (K1, p1) twice, * k3, p3, k1, p2, k3, rep from * to last 4 sts, (p1, k1) twice.
5th row: K4, * p2, Cr3B, k1, p1, C3F, p2, rep from * to last 4 sts, k4.
6th row: (K1, p1) twice, * k2, p3, k1, p1, k1, p2, k2, rep from * to last 4 sts,

(p1, k1) twice.
7th row: K4, * p1, Cr3B, (k1, p1) twice, C3F, p1, rep from * to last 4 sts, k4.
8th row: (K1, p1) twice, * k1, p3, (k1, p1) twice, k1, p2, k1, rep from * to last 4 sts, (p1, k1) twice.
9th row: K4, * Cr3B, (k1, p1) 3 times, C3F, rep from * to last 4 sts, k4.
10th row: (K1, p1) twice, * p3, (k1, p1) 3 times, k1, p2, rep from * to last 4 sts, (p1, k1) twice.
11th row: K6, (k1, p1) 4 times, * C4B, (k1, p1) 4 times, rep from * to last 6 sts, k6.
12th row: (K1, p1) twice, * p2, (k1, p1) 4 times, p2, rep from * to last 4 sts, (p1, k1) twice.
13th row: K4, * Cr3F, (k1, p1) 3 times, Cr3B, rep from * to last 4 sts, k4.
14th row: (K1, p1) twice, * k1, p2, (k1, p1) 3 times, p2, k1, rep from * to last 4 sts, (p1, k1) twice.
15th row: K4, * p1, Cr3F, (k1, p1) twice, Cr3B, p1, rep from * to last 4 sts, k4.
16th row: (K1, p1) twice, * k2, p2, (k1, p1) twice, p2, k2, rep from * to last 4 sts, (p1, k1) twice.
17th row: K4, * p2, Cr3F, k1, p1, Cr3B, p2, rep from * to last 4 sts, k4.
18th row: (K1, p1) twice, * k3, p2, k1, p3, k3, rep from * to last 4 sts, (p1, k1) twice.
19th row: K4, * p3, Cr3F, Cr3B, p3, rep from * to last 4 sts, k4.
20th row: As 2nd row.

Rep these 20 rows twice more, then 1st row once. Work should now measure 23 cm (9 in). Cast off.

To make the wide, horizontal strips —knit the following five times:
Using size 4 mm needles, cast on 54 sts.
1st row: K1, p2, k4, p2, (k2, p2) 9 times, p2, k4, p2, k1.
2nd row: K3, p4, k2, (k2, p2) 9 times, k2, p4, k3.
3rd row: K1, p2, C4F, p2, (p2, k2) 9 times, p2, C4F, p2, k1.
4th row: K3, p4, k2, (p2, k2) 9 times, k2, p4, k3.
5th row: As 1st row.
6th row: As 2nd row.

7th row: K1, p2, k4, p2, (p2, k2) 9 times, p2, k4, p2, k1.

8th row: As 4th row.

9th row: K1, p2, C4F, p2, (k2, p2) 9 times, p2, C4F, p2, k1.

10th row: As 2nd row.

11th row: As 7th row.

12th row: As 4th row.

These 12 rows form the pattern and are repeated. Continue in patt until work measures 183 cm (72 in) for double-bedspread or 137 cm (54 in) for single-bedspread, ending with a wrong side row. Cast off.

To make the narrower, top and bottom border strips — knit the following twice:

* Using size 4 mm needles, cast on 2 sts.

1st row: (P1, k1) into first st, k1.

2nd row: Sl 1, p1, k twice into last st.

3rd row: (P1, k1) into first st, k1, p1, k1.

4th row: Sl 1, k1, p2, k twice into last st.

5th row: (P1, k1) into first st, k1, p2, k2.

6th row: Sl 1, p1, k2, p2, k twice into last st.

7th row: (P1, k1) into first st, k1, p2, k2, p1, k1.

8th row: Sl 1, k1, p2, k2, p2, k twice into last st (10 sts).

Continue in double moss st as set, inc and working into patt 1 st at shaped edge on every row until there are 18 sts on the needle.

17th row: K twice into first st, k1, patt to end.

18th row: Patt 18, (p1, k1) into last st.

19th row: (K1, p1) into first st, k1, patt to end.

20th row: Patt 18, p1, k1, p twice into last st.

21st row: K twice into first st, k1, p1, k1, patt to end.

22nd row: Patt 18, p1, k1, p2, p twice into last st.

23rd row: (P1, k1) into first st, k3, p1, k1, patt to end.

24th row: Patt 18, p1, k1, p4, (k1, p1) into last st.

25th row: K twice into first st, p1, C4F, p1, k1, patt to end (27 sts).

26th row: Patt 18, p1, k1, p4, k1, p1, k1.

27th row: K2, p1, k4, p1, k1, patt to end.

28th row: Patt 18, p1, k1, p4, k1, p1, k1.

29th row: K2, p1, k4, p1, k1, patt to end.

30th row: Patt 18, p1, k1, p4, k1, p1, k1.

31st row: K2, p1, C4F, p1, k1, patt to end *

Rep last 6 rows until short edge of border measures 180.5 cm (71 in) for double-bedspread or 134.5 cm (53 in) for single-bedspread. Keeping continuity of patt and cable panel, dec 1 st at inner (cable) edge on every row until 2 sts remain. Cast off.

To make the narrower, side border strips — knit the following twice:

Work as for top and bottom borders from * to *. Rep last 6 rows until short edge of border measures 249 cm (98 in), ending with same patt row as top and bottom borders to start of shaping. Keeping continuity of patt and cable panel, dec 1 st at inner (cable) edge on every row until 2 sts remain. Cast off.

To make up a double bedspread:

Using a warm iron over a damp cloth, press all pieces lightly on the wrong side. Then, with a fine back stitch, join squares into six strips of eight squares, alternating the "sampler" patterns. For example, the first two strips will read: A, B, C, D, E, F, A, B and C,D,E,F,A,B,C,D. Sew the wide, horizontal strips to the strips of squares as shown in the photograph. Finally, sew on the narrower border strips, stitching the corner seams neatly. With a warm iron, press all the seams over a damp cloth.

To make up a single-bedspread:

Work exactly as for the double bedspread, except you will need to join the squares into six strips of six squares, alternating the "sampler" patterns so the first two strips read: A, B, C, D, E, F and B, C, D, E, F, A.

30

Pretty maids all in a row

Workaday clothes pegs, pipe-cleaners, a little paint and varnish, plus miscellaneous scraps from the rag-bag can add up to unusual and charming playthings.

When the vicar's children played with china dolls, most of his more humble parishioners were busy improvising toys for their children to play with. They were sitting by their doorsteps whittling bits of stick. Or commandeering wooden spoons from the kitchen which they painted with bright and funny faces. Or borrowing two-prong wooden pegs from the clothes-line to make into peg dolls very like those shown over the page.

The pegs were sold from door to door by itinerant pedlars and gypsies, and were cheap enough to fashion into engaging playthings. And as housewives never threw anything away, there were usually a few scraps of fabric to clothe them.

Today wooden pegs are getting harder to find because coloured plastic versions are taking over—to say nothing of indoor tumble driers. Some old-fashioned ironmongers still keep a stock. But most people have scraps of fabric they've hoarded; in fact half the fun of making these appealing toys is in using up unwanted offcuts that you haven't had the heart to put in the dustbin. It would be a shame to go out and buy anything specially.

However, as the dolls' faces play so vital a part, it could be worth investing in a sable paintbrush, which will be fine enough to ensure delicate work. Then you'll have no difficulty reproducing the quaint and slightly sur-

prised expressions they all wear.

Be sure to retain the scraped-back "hair"—it helps to impart a period flavour. If you're tempted to paint anything more ornate, or even stick on woollen hair, you'll lose the demure, Victorian mood.

The dolls' wardrobe, of course, will present no problem. The dresses are such a sheer delight to dream up, you may find the only difficulty you experience lies in restraining yourself from making peg dolls ad infinitum.

Materials

Traditional wooden two-prong clothes pegs (from the Handicraft Shop, direct or mail order).
Pipe-cleaners (from most tobacconist shops).
Some strong thread.
Poster paints (from art shops).
A small, good quality paintbrush (from art shops).
Clear varnish (from art shops—or you could use clear nail varnish if you have some handy).
9 cm ($3\frac{1}{2}$ in) deep broderie anglaise.
Any scraps of tiny-patterned printed cotton fabric.
Ribbon and trimming remnants.

Method

Paint the hair, face and shoes with poster paint. When all the colours are dry, give the entire peg a coat of clear varnish for protection.

Fold over the ends of the pipe-cleaners so they meet in the middle. Dip the folded "arms" into flesh-coloured paint and leave to dry.

To make the pantaloons: Cut two 5 cm (2 in) lengths of broderie anglaise, and with wrong sides together, make each piece into a tube, stitching up from the bottom for 6 cm (2½ in) only. Leave a minimal seam allowance of 3 mm (⅛ in). Turn the pantaloons right side out, and slide onto the doll's "legs" with the seams at inside-leg. Tuck in the raw edges at the doll's "chest" and "back", and gather in the top of the pantaloons with stitches.

To fix the arms: Place the pipe-cleaner arms round the back of the peg at "shoulder" height, and bind in place with strong thread. A few stitches through the pantaloons will help to keep the arms safely in place.

To make the sleeves and bodice: Select one of your printed cottons, and cut two 6 cm (2½ in) by 5 cm (2 in) pieces. With wrong sides together, and leaving a minimal seam allowance, stitch each piece into a tube, sewing along the 6 cm (2½ in) lengths for 3.5 cm (1⅜ in). Turn the sleeves right side out, and slip onto the doll's arms. Fold in the raw edges at the wrists, and gather in with stitches to fit. Fold in the raw edges over the shoulders, and secure with stitches where the sleeves meet at front and back to form bodice.

To make the skirt: Cut a 15 cm (6 in) by 10 cm (4 in) piece of matching printed cotton, and with wrong sides together, again leaving a minimal seam allowance, stitch along the 10 cm (4 in) length. Fold in the top edge, put on the doll, and gather into place with stitches around the waist. Secure the skirt to the bodice with a few more stitches. Hem the bottom of the skirt (unless a selvedge can be used) to leave the black-shod feet and a flash of frilly pantaloon showing.

Finally, add a lace collar, a narrow sash and a prim little apron.

31

A jugful of Summer for all the year round

**Small-scale dots, checks and diamonds
form the disciplined background for unruly
nasturtiums in this stylish picture. Unexpected
composition, with the jug off-centre,
lends spontaneity and freshness.**

Our picture, which we show smaller than actual size in the photograph, quite cleverly combines embroidery and appliqué. However, as the embroidery demands much skill and patience, to say nothing of taking up lots of time, you might prefer to make a simplified version. You could, for instance, appliqué the window and window sill, instead of working them laboriously in single-strand satin stitch. Or you could appliqué the jug instead of embroidering it—a terra cotta-coloured felt would be ideal as it would give a rough-textured pottery effect. But if you can spare the time to embroider the picture fully, you'll not only have proved yourself an expert needlewoman, but you'll be rewarded with something for future generations to treasure.

Materials

Anchor stranded embroidery cottons in the following colours: 022, 046, 047, 0134, 0139, 0216, 0225, 0242, 0264, 0268, 0278, 0291, 0292, 0297, 0302, 0313, 0323, 0332, 0334 and 0397.

A piece of unbleached calico, 25 cm ($9\frac{3}{4}$ in) by 30 cm ($11\frac{3}{4}$ in), to form the picture's background.

A small strip of cream lawn to form the window blind.

A piece of small-scale checked fabric, about 20 cm (8 in) square, to form the curtains and tablecloth. (It's important to stick to tiny checks which create a neat and sophisticated mood. Any softer pattern, particularly a floral, would blur the impact of the design.)

Size 10 crewel needles.

About 110 cm (43 in) of 1.25 cm ($\frac{1}{2}$ in) wide white cotton tape.

Strong thread.

An embroidery hoop.

(All the above materials from John Lewis and John Lewis Partnership stores.)

Copydex.

A piece of thin cream card, 14 cm ($5\frac{1}{2}$ in) wide by 18 cm (7 in) long.

A craft knife (available from craft or art shops).

Method

Using a ruler and a craft knife, cut a 9.5 cm ($3\frac{3}{4}$ in) wide by 13.5 cm ($5\frac{3}{8}$ in) long rectangle from the piece of cream card. This will leave you with your mount. You will find it helps to place the mount over the picture from time to time, to check that everything is correctly positioned.

To trace the design: Stretch the calico tightly in the embroidery hoop so that the grain is straight. Using the photograph as a guide, draw the design onto the calico in pencil, omitting the vase, the flowers, the leaves and the blindcord and ring. Practise on a piece of paper first if you're nervous, but really, it's an extremely simple design to tackle. Slip a small thick book under

the calico to provide a firm base.

To embroider the window sill and wallpaper: Using one strand of 0139, work the upright window bar and the window sill in satin stitch, as shown in Diagram 4, and the bottom of the window in long and short stitch, as shown in Diagram 5, extending the embroidery 4 mm ($\frac{3}{16}$ in) beyond the outer margin of the picture. Work the lines on the window panes in stem stitch, as shown in Diagram 2, using one strand of 0397. Using one strand of 0292, sew the French knots, shown in Diagram 1, that form the pattern on the dotted wallpaper below the window.

To make the window blind: Cut the blind from the small strip of cream lawn, allowing a 2.5 cm (1 in) margin at top and sides, and a 4 mm ($\frac{3}{16}$ in) turning at the bottom edge. Iron under the 4 mm ($\frac{3}{16}$ in) turning to form a hem, and machine with tiny stitches. Pin and tack into position on the calico. Remove the calico from the embroidery hoop, and machine with zig-zag stitch around the top and sides of the blind, 2 cm ($\frac{3}{4}$ in) from the edge of the picture. Replace the calico in the hoop, making sure that the grain is still straight, and place the card mount over the picture to check that the blind is correctly positioned.

To make the curtains and table-cloth: Cut the check curtains on the straight, but cut the tablecloth on the bias, so the checks become diamonds. In both cases, allow a 2.5 cm (1 in) margin around the outer edges, and a 6 mm ($\frac{1}{4}$ in) turning at any inner edges that show in the picture. Iron under the 6 mm ($\frac{1}{4}$ in) turnings to form hems. Glue (or appliqué if preferred) the curtains and tablecloth into position on the calico. Again, place the card mount over the picture to check positioning.

To embroider the jug: Draw the outline of the vase onto the tablecloth, extending it about 2 mm ($\frac{1}{8}$ in) above the overlap of the flowers. Using two strands of 0134, work a row of chain stitch, as shown in Diagram 7, to form the base of the jug, and then cover the chain stitch with sloping satin stitch. This will give a raised effect so the bottom rim of the jug stands out realistically. Work the jug handle in the same way, so it looks thick and three-dimensional. Using one strand of 0134, outline the body of the jug in split stitch, as shown in Diagram 3, and fill in with vertical rows of split stitch following the curvaceous shape of the jug. When completed, the jug will have a richly-textured and "roughcast" surface.

To work the flowers, stems and leaves: Using pencil, draw onto the "wallpaper" and "tablecloth" the outline of the flowers, leaves and stems. Then working in tight stem stitch and with a single strand, outline them all, at the same time adding the outlines of the flowers and leaves that grow up against the window sill or hang down over the jug. Consult the photograph for appropriate colours throughout. Now start filling everything in with embroidery. Fill in the leaves with circular buttonhole stitch, as shown in Diagram 6, starting from the centre, and adding leaf-veins in 0264. Treat each flower petal separately, working from the outside towards the middle in concentric lines of small stem stitches. Work the flower spurs similarly in 0278, and fill in any unwanted gaps that may have arisen with 0268. Add any stems that have been covered in 0242. Work the centres of all the flowers with small single stitches in 022 and 0332.

To finish off: Positioning it by eye, stitch the pull-ring for the blind. Work it in small chain stitches using one strand of 0292, and to make it stand out in relief, whip over the chain stitches with regularly-spaced overcast stitches, taking care not to pierce the "window sill" behind.

To add the pull-cord, stitch one

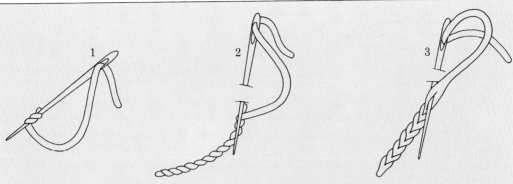

Diagram 1 To make a French knot, the needle is twisted several times around the thread, turned and inserted into the hole from which it emerged.

Diagram 2 Stem stitch is worked with the thread kept on the same side of the needle.

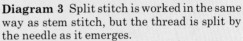

Diagram 3 Split stitch is worked in the same way as stem stitch, but the thread is split by the needle as it emerges.

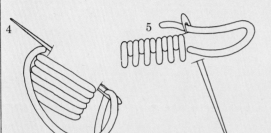

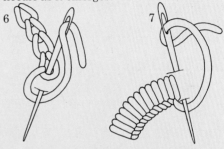

Diagram 4 Satin stitch can be worked in varying lengths, but for this embroidery, even lengths are mostly needed.

Diagram 5 To work long and short stitch, do the first row in long and short satin stitch, as shown, but do subsequent rows in satin stitches of even lengths.

Diagram 6 Buttonhole stitch is always worked from left to right. Pack the stitches as closely together as possible.

Diagram 7 To work chain stitch, the needle is inserted into the hole from which it has emerged to make the next stitch.

strand of 0292 to the centre-hem of the blind, pass it just under the top of the pull-ring and bring it out on the back of the picture. Take the strand up to the top of the picture-back, check its tension on the front, and stitch.

Finally, remove the completed picture from the hoop. Pin the white cotton tape all round the calico, so the edge of the tape does not extend beyond the edge of the calico. Using strong thread, machine in place with three rows of zig-zags. Now that the calico edges have been reinforced, lay the embroidered picture face down, and lay the cream card mount over it, with inside edges framing the worked area of the calico and outside edges parallel with the calico edges. Mark round the outside of the mount onto the calico with pencil, and remove the mount. Cut a piece of stout backing card to fit into the pencilled marks, lay it onto the back of the calico, and pull the calico edges over the stout card. Using strong thread, lace the picture tightly, first from side to side and then from top to bottom, adjusting as you go. Mount picture and frame it. We used an old and much-painted frame from a junk shop, which we stripped back to the natural wood for a simple finish. This played up the natural simplicity of our picture—anything too ornate would have swamped it. The inner measurements were 14 cm (5½ in) wide by 18 cm (7 in) long: it helps if you find a suitable frame first.

32

Beautifully pure and natural

Homemade beauty treatments are much cheaper than shop-bought products, and it's nice to have the reassuring knowledge that they're full of good and healthy things.

Nature didn't mean us to live in centrally-heated homes or bake our skins in the pursuit of a suntan. But, fortunately nature did provide us with several easily available ingredients to help repair the self-inflicted damage. Their moisturising and nourishing properties go a long way towards solving common beauty problems like dry skin, brittle nails and dull, parched hair. So here's a whole host of beauty recipes.

Gentle neck cream

Ingredients

50 g (2 oz) of white beeswax (direct or mail order from John Bell & Croyden —minimum amount 100 g (4 oz)).
2 tablespoonfuls of anhydrous lanoline (also from John Bell & Croyden —minimum amount 100 g (4 oz)).
$\frac{1}{2}$ cup of avocado oil (from wholefood and health shops).
2 teaspoonfuls of liquid honey.
A dash of your favourite scent.

Method

Melt the beeswax, lanoline and oil together in a double boiler. Remove from the heat and stir until cool. Add the honey, mix well, then add the scent. Decant into small screwtop jars.

We used the jar the anhydrous lanoline came in, an old cold cream jar, and a jar that once held Elsenham liqueur marmalade.

We stuck on labels you can buy at most stationers, inscribed them using a thick-nibbed italic pen, and added adhesive floral transfers by Decalomania (supplied in packs, direct or mail order, from Paperchase). As nearly all the following recipes are for immediate use, they don't need any kind of packaging.

Banana face mask

Banana contains vitamin A, and is just the right consistency for making into a nourishing face mask. This recipe is for skins that have become very dry and dehydrated.

Ingredients

1 small ripe banana, or half a large one.
30 ml (2 tablespoonfuls) of olive oil.

Method

Mash and sieve the banana. Warm the olive oil and beat into the banana a drop at a time. Apply all over the face and neck, avoiding the eye area. Leave on for fifteen minutes to half a' hour, and then rinse off.

For skins that are normal to dry, use the same amount of banana, but instead of adding olive oil, add 5 ml (one teaspoonful) of liquid honey and 10 ml (two teaspoonfuls) of cream, and mix well together.

For skin that is oily down the centre, follow the recipe for normal to dry

skin, but add 5 ml (one teaspoonful) of orange juice. This has a slightly astringent effect, which is beneficial to the oily centre strip without harming the drier skin either side.

Avocado nail cream

Avocado pear is rich in protein, and provides an effective treatment for that most irritating of problems—brittle or flaking nails.

Ingredients

5 ml (1 teaspoonful) of avocado.
5 ml (1 teaspoonful) of liquid honey.
5 ml (1 teaspoonful) of egg yolk.
A pinch of sea salt.

Method

Mix all the ingredients, rub well into the nails and surrounding area, leave for half an hour and rinse off.

Avocado also provides an excellent conditioner for hair that is permanently dry, or has become temporarily dry through over-exposure to sunlight. Just mash or sieve half an avocado, and apply to the hair, rubbing it well into the ends. Wrap the hair in a towel to keep in the heat from the scalp—this encourages the hair to soak up the goodness. Leave on for at least an hour, and then shampoo as usual. Add a little lemon juice to the last rinse if your hair is fair; a little cider vinegar if your hair is mousey to dark.

For a coconut milk facial

Coconut milk has such soothing and softening properties, it would be marvellous to be able to suggest filling the bath full of it, and letting every square inch of skin soak up the benefit. But here are two more realistic suggestions. If your skin is prone to blackheads, coconut milk will help soften the sebum that causes blocked pores. Simply heat the milk of one coconut until it's lukewarm. Pour into a bowl, and use to splash the face, over and over again, for ten minutes or so. Or alternatively, hold a milk-soaked sponge to the "problem" areas.

If your skin has become roughened with wind or friction, heat half a cupfull of coconut milk until lukewarm, and then add one tablespoonful of fine oatmeal. Mix well, and apply to the areas of roughened skin, whether on the face, the elbows, the knees or back of heels. Leave on for ten to fifteen minutes and rinse off.

Lime body lotion

This is ideal for skin that is always dry, or has toughened up through too much sun.

Ingredients

30 ml (2 tablespoonfuls) of freshly squeezed lime juice.
45 ml (3 tablespoonfuls) of rose water.
15 ml (1 tablespoonful) of glycerine.

Method

Make some rose water by filling a saucepan with the red petals of any heavily scented roses, adding a little water, and bringing to the boil. Allow to cool with the lid still on, and strain when cold. Mix three tablespoonfuls of the rose water with the lime juice and glycerine until the ingredients have a smooth consistency. As the lotion will keep for three days in the fridge, rub it into the dry skin daily.

Lemon sunburn lotion

If your face or body has been exposed to too much sun, a lemon lotion will help soothe the sunburnt areas and take some of the stinging heat out of the skin.

Ingredients

1 lemon.
1 egg white.

Method

Squeeze the lemon and add the juice to the egg white. Whisk well, and transfer into a small saucepan. Stir the mixture over a low heat until it thickens, allow to cool, and apply to the stricken areas. As lemon has important revitalising properties, this makes it suitable for many skin and hair remedies.

A lemon face mask will help tone and tighten a slack skin, for instance. Just mix 30 ml (two tablespoonfuls) of lemon juice with 15 ml (one tablespoonful) of Fuller's Earth, until you have achieved a smooth consistency. Apply to the face, avoiding the eyes, leave on for ten to fifteen minutes, and rinse off.

A lemon leg wax will enable you to remove unwanted hair in an effective and sweet-smelling way—although it's advisable to have waxing done professionally before attempting to do it yourself at home. Simply squeeze the juice of two lemons into a small saucepan, add 500 g (1 lb 2 oz) of granulated sugar, and heat slowly until the sugar melts and the mixture turns golden brown. Remove from the heat, and add 7.5 ml (1½ teaspoonfuls) of glycerine. By the time you have mixed the glycerine well in, the wax should be the right temperature for use.

Apple skin tonic

Apple is rich in pectin, and helps to rebalance, revitalise and invigorate all types of skin.

Ingredients

½ a peeled apple.
30 ml (2 tablespoonfuls) of liquid honey.

Method

Mash and sieve the apple. Combine with the honey and beat well. Apply to the face and neck, avoiding the eye area. Leave on for ten to fifteen minutes and rinse off.

Pear face mask

Pear has disinfectant, astringent properties, and makes a perfect face mask for a spotty skin.

Ingredients

½ a ripe pear.
5 ml (1 teaspoonful) of powdered milk.

Method

Mash and sieve the pear and mix to a smooth consistency with the powdered milk. Avoiding the eyes, apply to the spotty parts of the face only, to help dry up the spots. Leave on for ten to fifteen minutes and rinse off.

Used on its own, pear also makes a good face mask for oily skin, because of its astringent qualities. Just mash and sieve half a ripe pear, apply to the face avoiding the eye area, leave on for fifteen minutes and rinse off.

Herbal hair rinse for normal hair

Dried rosemary makes a refreshing hair rinse for mousey to dark hair; dried camomile brings out the highlights of fair hair. It's best to make several rinse sachets at a time, storing them in any attractive jar that has an air-tight lid. The cork-topped jar filled with dried lavender in our photograph would make a pretty container, especially with an inscribed label.

Make some sachets (these are not shown in the photograph) by cutting 5 cm (2 in) squares of muslin or cheese-cloth. Put a teaspoonful of dried rosemary or camomile in the centre of each square, and tie the squares into a bundle with a piece of cotton. When you need a hair rinse, place one of the sachets in 600 ml (1 pint) of already boiling water, remove from the heat, and leave to cool.

For a scented bath bag

The little lavender bags in our photograph are meant for hanging from a bath tap, so the hot water flows through them and becomes permeated with fragrance. Of course, you can use other ingredients if you want a different scent—perhaps a mixture of orange blossom, lime blossom and eau de cologne mint—but really anything with a good smell will fit the bill.

The bags themselves are very easy to make. Cut two small squares from scraps of tiny-printed fabric, using pinking shears to give a decorative edge. Stitch wrong sides together along three sides.

Buy a 70 cm (28 in) length of narrow ribbon, and about 1.5 cm (⅝ in) down from the top of the bag, stitch the ribbon to both sides of the bag, about 13 cm (5 in) in from each end of ribbon.

Fill the bag with dried lavender or whatever you may have preferred. Tie the 13 cm (5 in) ribbon-ends tightly to one side of the bag with a single knot. This will close the neck of the bag securely. Then tie the ribbon-ends to the other side and finish with a bow. The central portion of ribbon will form a loop for tap-hanging.

33

Sumptuous scalloped and satin-bound towels

**Just add satin bias binding to ordinary
terry towelling, and you'll find you've added
instant glamour. We defy anyone to use
these towels without feeling pampered,
cherished and expensive.**

Quite why a simple trim of satin should turn dull necessities into sybaritic luxuries is one of the minor mysteries of life. But there is one rule: keep colours matching. If you trim things in a contrasting satin, you'll find the results look brash and vulgar. So unless you're sticking to the colours we show, check there's a matching binding before buying the towelling.

Materials

Towelling by the metre, 90 cm (36 in) wide. In silver-grey, you'll need a piece 140 cm (55 in) long; in cream, 65 cm ($25\frac{1}{2}$ in) long; in white, 65 cm ($25\frac{1}{2}$ in) long—this will be enough to make two white towels.

2 cm ($\frac{3}{4}$ in) wide Wearwell acetate satin bias binding by Berisfords. (All from John Lewis and John Lewis Partnership stores).

Method

Wash the towelling first in case of shrinkage. Cut a paper pattern for the scallops, making it three scallops wide. Each scallop should measure 15 cm (6 in) wide at the top and 5.5 cm ($2\frac{1}{4}$ in) deep from top to bottom.

The silver-grey towel.
If the selvedges on either side of the towelling are too big to take the satin binding, trim them down a little. Pin your paper pattern onto the bottom raw edge of the towelling, and cut out

three scallops. Move the pattern along, pin, and cut out the remaining three scallops. Open out the top fold of the bias binding, and with right side against the towelling, so both edges line up, pin in place all around. Machine so the stitches fall along the crease of the opened-out binding. You will need to lift the foot of the machine to change direction at the top of each scallop, and will find that the excess binding falls into a natural pleat as you work. Pull the binding over the edges, and leaving the bottom fold of the bias binding folded, hem neatly along the other side of the towelling.

The cream towel.
We made a 90 cm (36 in) wide by 65 cm ($25\frac{1}{2}$ in) deep towel, so that once again, the selvedges came at the sides, and the six scallops were cut from the bottom raw edge.

But if you wanted a more conventionally shaped towel, you could buy the towelling only 60 cm ($23\frac{1}{2}$ in) long, and use the 90 cm (36 in) width as the length; the 60 cm ($23\frac{1}{2}$ in) length as the width. Then you would cut four scallops from the bottom selvedge edge.

The white towel.
Cut the 90 cm (36 in) wide by 65 cm ($25\frac{1}{2}$ in) long piece of towelling down the middle. Take one piece, and cut three scallops from the 45 cm ($17\frac{1}{2}$ in) wide bottom raw edge.

34

The green leaves of Summer

**These leaf-shaped cushions could become the
russet or golden leaves of autumn if you chose
the satin in a different colour.
Whichever season you prefer, they'll
guarantee a snazzy impact.**

Most satin cushions are little and fussy. They belong to that irritating class of scatter-cushions that deserve to get scattered all over the floor because they provide nothing at all in the way of comfort. But our handsome cushions are big enough to offer really substantial support. The oak leaf measures 70 cm (27½ in) long by 41 cm (16 in) wide; the ivy leaf measures 52 cm (20½ in) from tip to stem and 71 cm (28 in) at its widest point; and the honeysuckle leaf measures 71 cm (28 in) long by 37 cm (14½ in) at its widest point. They'll look spectacular grouped together on a sofa, or stunning on an armchair in splendid isolation. And if you live cooped up in a town they'll bring in a breath of the great outdoors.

Materials

2.5 m of Epsom satin, 90 cm (36 in) wide.

2.5 m of medium weight polyester wadding, 90 cm (36 in) wide.

1.75 m of bleached calico, 137 cm (54 in) wide.

2.5 m of muslin, 90 cm (36 in) wide.

1 bag of foam chips (quite apart from the expense, real feather would fly everywhere and prove impossible to handle).

A 40.5 cm (16 in) zip.

Thread to match the satin.

Buttonhole twist to match the satin. (All from John Lewis or John Lewis Partnership stores).

3 large sheets of newspaper.

A pair of dressmaking scissors.

A pair of sharp, small scissors.

Method

To cut out the paper patterns: In the drawing over the page, the leaf outlines are drawn on graph paper, with each square of the graph representing 5 cm (2 in). The honeysuckle leaf is at the top left, the oak leaf at the top right, and the ivy leaf at the bottom.

To transfer the leaf outlines to your sheets of newspaper, first turn the newspapers into graph paper by drawing lines at 5 cm (2 in) intervals across them in both directions. Then, closely referring over the page, draw in the leaf outlines so they take up the same number of squares on your newspapers as on our graph paper. Cut two identical leaf shapes for the oak, two for the honeysuckle and two for the ivy.

As there is only just enough satin to make the three cushion covers, arrange all the patterns on the satin first. Do not follow the spacing shown in our drawing because this is only accurate for the actual leaf outlines. But you will find you can cut the two oak leaf patterns and the two honeysuckle leaf patterns from 1.5 m of fabric; the two ivy leaf patterns from 1 m of fabric.

To make up a leaf: If you start with the oak leaf, pin the oak leaf patterns

to the satin (making sure to reverse one so you have a front and a back), cut out the two leaf shapes, and before you unpin them, tack-mark in all the leaf veins. Then cut out two leaf shapes from the wadding and two from the muslin.

Next, place one of the wadding leaf shapes on the wrong side of a satin leaf shape and put one of the muslin leaf shapes on top. Holding them firmly together, tack securely through all three layers.

Thread your sewing machine with ordinary thread in the spool but with buttonhole twist in the upper part of the machine. Carefully sew along the vein lines. Repeat to make the second side of the oak leaf.

Putting in the zip: With the right sides of the leaves together, machine around them 5 cm (2 in) either side of the zip notches, which are shown in our drawing, and 1.5 cm ($\frac{5}{8}$ in) in from the edge, using ordinary thread only this time. Between the notches, cut away 1.5 cm ($\frac{5}{8}$ in) from the seam allowance of the wadding and the muslin, and tack back the satin seam allowance to the wrong side. Using a dry-iron, press lightly into position with the setting on silk.

Now machine-stitch the zip between the notches, working one side at a time from the right side. Dry-iron with the setting on silk.

To make up the cushion cover: Leaving the zip half open, and with right sides together, machine-stitch around the rest of the cushion 1.5 cm ($\frac{5}{8}$ in) from the edge, still using ordinary thread. To neaten the edge, machine a line of zig-zag stitch next to the line of machine stitching inside the seam allowance. Then cut away the excess.

With a small pair of sharp scissors, cut V-shaped notches on the curves at right angles to the line of machine stitches, taking great care not to cut through the stitching. Turn the cushion cover through to the right side. Make the honeysuckle and ivy leaf cushion covers in exactly the same way as for the oak leaf.

To make a stalk: Cut a piece of newspaper 9 cm ($3\frac{1}{2}$ in) square to provide a pattern for the stalk. Pin the pattern to a satin offcut, and cut out. Unpin, and with right sides together, fold the satin in half along the grain. Machine together along the longest edge only, working 1.5 cm ($\frac{5}{8}$ in) from the raw edge. You will now have a tube shape. Trim the seam allowance to neaten.

At one end of the tube, fold the raw edges back 1.5 cm ($\frac{5}{8}$ in). Then, on the right side of a scrap of satin, and using a pencil, draw round a 1p piece, and cut out a circle 1 cm ($\frac{3}{8}$ in) bigger all round, to give a seam allowance. With all wrong sides showing, hand-sew the 1p piece circle to the turned-back end of the tube. Trim the seam allowance, and pull the tube through to the right side. Finally, fold under the raw edges of the other end of the tube 1.5 cm ($\frac{5}{8}$ in), and stuff it with foam chips. When full, hand-sew neatly to the cushion cover.

To make the inner cushion: So that the cushion covers can be removed for cleaning, we made calico inner cushions as follows:

Trim one of the newspaper patterns to the inner outline shown in the drawing. Fold the calico in half, pin the oak leaf newspaper pattern to it, and cut out both leaf shapes in one go. With right sides together, machine-stitch round the edges, 1.5 cm ($\frac{5}{8}$ in) in, leaving a 15 cm (6 in) gap on a straight part of the leaf. Trim the seam allowances, and with a small, sharp pair of scissors, cut V-shaped notches on the curves of the leaf at right angles to the machine stitches, taking care not to cut the actual stitching. Turn through to the right side, stuff with the foam chips, and neatly hand sew the 15 cm (6 in) gap together. Repeat in exactly the same way for the honeysuckle and ivy leaf shapes.

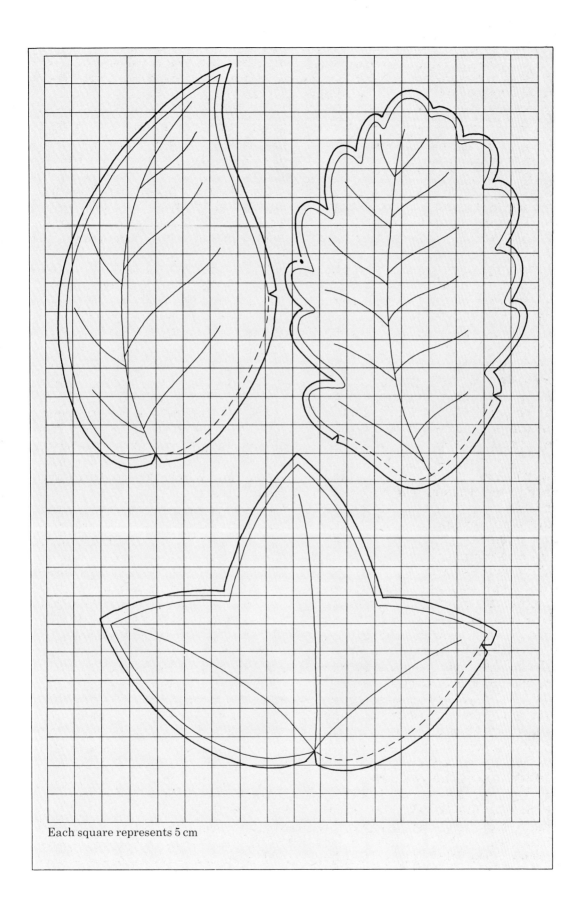

Each square represents 5 cm

35

Dreamy sleep pillows

Whether you make them with soporific hops or herbs, or use a filling of flower-petal pot pourri, these pillows will give you fragrant nights.

Small lavender bags and sachets are so easy to make, it's quite likely you tried them as a child. And our sleep pillows can be almost as easy—that intricate be-ribboning is surprisingly simple—and if you buy the ready-mixed herbs or pot pourri from a shop, you can finish them in double-quick time. But if you have a thriving garden that makes you long to capture its fleeting scents, we suggest ways of exploiting it to the full. We give a basic recipe for flower petal pot pourri and tell you how to mix your own herbs. But now, for how you can make a really dreamy sleep pillow.

We give details for one 23 cm (9 in) square, but you can make it larger or smaller as you fancy. And with luck, your scrap bag will supply most of your needs.

Materials

Two pieces of muslin (or cheesecloth or organdie), 23 cm (9 in) square.

Two pieces of any pretty cotton fabric, 23 cm (9 in) square.

One piece of iron-on Vilene, about 20 cm (8 in) square.

Leftover ribbon lengths.

Leftovers of lace or broderie anglaise trimming.

Tiny embroidered rose-sprigs (from haberdashery departments of most stores).

50 g (2 oz) of ready-spiced sleep herbs (from Meadow Herbs, direct or mail

order) or a bag of hops or 25 g (1 oz) of ready-spiced pot pourri (both direct or mail order from Culpeper).

Two 20 cm (8 in) squares of thick cotton-wool, from an unfolded roll. (This will be unnecessary if you are using herbs from your garden.)

Method

Take the two squares of muslin, and stitch together round three sides, snipping at the corners before turning right side out. This gives you an inner bag to take the filling. If you're supplying your own herbs or pot pourri, you'll be able to stuff the bag generously full. If not, make the most of shop-bought supplies by combining them with the cotton-wool.

To eke out shop-bought ingredients: Carefully tear each square of cotton-wool into two layers, making four squares in all. Create a "sandwich" by sprinkling the herbs or pot pourri onto three of the layers, and topping with the fourth cotton-wool layer. Oversew round the edges, and slip into the muslin bag. Whichever way you've filled the muslin bag, now oversew its fourth side.

To create the ribbon lattice-work: Place the Vilene, shiny side up, on a soft but firm surface. The carpet is likely to be the handiest. Lay two ribbons upon the Vilene so they cross at the centre, and fix at the ends with pins pushed upright through the Vilene into the carpet. (If ribbons have a right and a wrong side, be sure to place them wrong side down on the Vilene.) Then weave the other ribbons in and out, fixing all the ends with upright pins. Tack the ribbon-ends to the edge of the Vilene and remove pins. Place the work (making sure the ribbons are lying flat) face downwards onto the ironing board, and iron the Vilene onto the backs of the ribbons.

To make up the sleep pillow: Place the ribbon-covered Vilene right side up on one of the squares of cotton fab-ric, and stitch together round all the edges. Place the ribbon-covered square of cotton fabric upon the other square of cotton fabric, right sides together, and stitch round three edges. Neaten the seams, snip the corners, and turn right side out.

Slip in the fragrance-filled muslin pillow, turn in the open edges, and oversew the fourth edge. Trim with a frill of lace or broderie anglaise.

To make your own pot pourri: Pot pourri is a blend of dried petals, flowers, aromatic herbs, a mixture of spices, and a fixative. The fixative is absolutely vital, because it seals the fragrance and makes it last longer. Most people also add essential oils for good measure. These are natural extracts from plants, but if you pick your flowers and leaves under ideal conditions, you may be able to do without them.

What to pick: Rose petals make a good basis for pot pourri, especially red ones, which have a stronger scent. Then you can pick almost anything perfumed your garden has to offer, using it in smaller proportions. Suitable flowers include pinks, carnations, lavender, lily of the valley, orange blossom, jasmine, honeysuckle, wallflowers and violets. It's best to avoid any fleshy flowers because they don't dry very successfully.

Next, pick a medley of aromatic leaves and herbs, gathering enough to make one part to seven parts of petals and flowers. Anything from the following plants will serve well: scented geraniums, camomile, nasturtium, sweet bay, lemon verbena, sweet cicely, thyme, sage, rosemary, eau-de-cologne, mint, balm and tarragon.

Although there are so many possibilities to choose from, it's wisest to stick to only about six.

How to pick: With the exception of lavender, which should be picked when the flowers are beginning to fade, gather all the flowers when the blooms are on the point of opening or have only just opened. This saves the essential oils, an important factor because they give off perfume. The best time to pick is around mid-morning, when any dew has evaporated, and the plants are quite dry.

Leaves are also most highly scented when the flowers on the plants are just about to open, so pick them at this time. Seek out young, thin leaf shoots, but gather them sparingly to avoid weakening the plants. Herbs, like leaves, should always be picked early on a dry day.

How to dry: Spread out the petals, leaves and herbs in separate layers, if possible on trays made by stretching muslin or old net curtains over empty boxes or frames; otherwise on sheets of paper. Place them in a well-ventilated, dry atmosphere, and leave for five days, turning daily, until they become crisp and almost paper-dry. As slow drying is essential, don't put them in the airing cupboard unless it is cool. When dry, store in any container with an air-tight lid, like an old enamel bread bin, a stone crock or perhaps a plastic bin.

How to make the spice mixture: This can vary according to inspiration and the contents of your store cupboard, but obviously it will be most successful if you fresh-crush the ingredients in a pestle and mortar instead of buying them ready powdered. The following mixture would provide enough for about four pints of petals, leaves and herbs.

Dry the thinly pared rinds of an orange and lemon on a baking tray in a cool oven. When quite hard, put through a blender or mincer to reduce them to a fine powder. Mix the powdered rinds with 25 g (1 oz) of bruised coriander seeds, 25 g (1 oz) of grated nutmeg, 25 g (1 oz) of whole bruised cloves, two to three sticks of roughly bruised cinnamon (or 25 g (1 oz) of powdered cinnamon), and a sliced eighth of a vanilla pod. Smell the mixture as you go along, and adjust the quantities to suit your taste.

How to make up the pot pourri: Add 50 g (2 oz) of fixative to the spice mixture. If dedicated, you can make your own by drying and grinding the root of angelica; or drying and grinding the rhizome of sweet flag. But most people buy ready-powdered orris root, which derives from the imported rhizome of Florentine iris. This is available, direct or mail order, from both Culpeper and Meadow Herbs. If you are using essential oils (also from both Culpeper and Meadow Herbs), add them to the spice mixture too.

Now sprinkle the spice mixture and fixative into the container of dried petals, leaves and herbs, making sure it's distributed evenly throughout. Replace the lid on the container, and leave for a few days before putting in your sleep pillow.

NB The dry pot pourri we have described is best for use in sachets and sleep pillows, but if you want to use pot pourri in open bowls to scent a room, it's better to make a moist, and stronger scented version. This is made in almost exactly the same way, except that you put 100 g (4 oz) of crushed sea salt in layers between the dried petals and leaves as you add the spice mixture, sprinkle on a few drops of rose water, and leave for four to five weeks before using. As moist pot pourri is going to be on view, you can add some brightly coloured but unscented dried flowers to provide visual interest.

To mix sleep herbs: Hops have such a pungent smell they only need drying and they're ready for use, but any mixture of herbs will need a fixative.

For a simple sleep pillow filling, you could just add orris root and possibly an essential oil, but if you have the time and the ingredients, you will probably enjoy much sweeter dreams if you also add the pot pourri spice mixture.

36–46

Some sheer temptation

Everyday cooking can get very boring, but it's different devising special treats. They're exciting to make, a delight to display and irresistably good to eat.

These delectable dainties are full of good things; and although some of the ingredients are admittedly expensive, they still work out at a fraction of the price you'd have to pay in a luxury shop. They make fresher and better eating too, and if you set them out in sumptuous array, they'll look more attractive than any window display.

In fact, half the fun lies in presenting them well. Hunt out lots of little dishes and bowls—they'll be all the more appealing if they mix instead of match. You can often find lovely ones at jumble sales, cast out because they're odd, not because they're damaged. Jumble sales are a good source of small wicker baskets too, though with luck you may still have one that once held flowers. Make use of any "useless" boxes you've been hoarding. And even plunder the kitchen for suitable containers—sturdy casseroles have a handsome simplicity and ordinary glass storage jars are ideal, because they show their tempting contents clearly. Pay a longer than usual visit to your local stationers, particularly any branch of W. H. Smith. You may find they sell the miniature sweet cases that give our truffles such a professional finish. And they're sure to sell paper doilys—indispensable for making plain containers look pretty.

If you can bear to part with any of your handiwork, all of the goodies in our photograph would make perfect

gifts. And as they're so special you need only give a few. They'll look more expensive in "exclusive" quantities. It's worth taking pains to present the gifts well; and it's always wise to label the contents, telling people how long they will last. Pages 46–51 are full of ideas on how to wrap things to full advantage. And if possible, visit a branch of Paperchase or send off for their catalogue. Paperchase is an unbeatable source, not only of incredibly beautiful wrapping papers, which you could use to cover plain cardboard boxes, but of miniature carrier bags, pretty cardboard boxes, and unusual imported labels and gift tags. A nice touch, if you've tied a box with ribbon, is to copy the practice of French sweet shops and patisseries. There, assistants leave the ends of the knot or bow extra long and then stretch them out with a pair of scissors. When freed, they spring back into corkscrew curls. *All teaspoonfuls are level unless otherwise specified.*

36 Almond butter macaroons

These are mouth-watering eaten with coffee, slipped into a trifle, or served with a fruity dessert or chocolate mousse. Stored in an airtight container, they'll keep for up to a fortnight, so it's worth baking a reasonable batch. Our recipe makes about 48.

Ingredients

1 egg white.
75 g (3 oz) of ground almonds.
100 g (4 oz) of caster sugar.
2.5 ml ($\frac{1}{2}$ teaspoonful) of almond essence.
A few flaked almonds.
A few glace cherries.

Method

Whisk the egg white until stiff, and then fold in the ground almonds, the caster sugar and the almond essence. Spoon the mixture into a fabric forcing bag fitted with a 1 cm ($\frac{1}{2}$ in) plain vegetable nozzle. Pipe out in small blobs on a baking sheet lined with non-stick paper, making sure to keep them apart. Pop pieces of flaked almonds on half the macaroons, and bake the entire batch at 180°C (350°F), gas mark 4, for about 15 minutes or until just starting to colour. While still warm, decorate the plain macaroons with pieces of glace cherry. Cool slightly, ease off the paper, and cool on a wire rack.

37 Scotch butter tablet

This is a meltingly smooth, rich-tasting fudge. Closely wrapped in Cling film, it will keep for a couple of weeks—or much longer if you put it in the freezer. Our recipe makes about 450 g (1 lb).

Ingredients

450 g (1 lb) of sugar.
100 g (4 oz) of butter.
150 ml ($\frac{1}{4}$ pint) of evaporated milk.
150 ml ($\frac{1}{4}$ pint) of ordinary milk.
A few drops of vanilla essence.

Method

Grease a shallow tin, 15 cm (6 in) square, and set aside. Place the sugar, butter, undiluted evaporated milk and fresh milk into a heavy 2.8 litre (5 pint) saucepan. Heat gently to dissolve the sugar, stirring occasionally. Every grain of sugar must be clear before you start boiling. Bring the saucepan to the boil and boil steadily until the mixture reaches 116°C (240°F)—the "soft ball" stage. Agitate occasionally. Take off the heat and place on a cool metal surface. Add a few drops of vanilla essence and beat well until the mixture becomes thick and creamy, showing signs of graining.

Pour at once into the greased tin, scraping the sides of the saucepan with a wooden spatula, and washing the pan in water immediately, before any traces of fudge set solid and spoil the finish. When nearly cold, mark the Scotch butter tablet into squares with a knife, using a sawing motion.

38 Ginger chocolate cups

These velvety-textured and delectable morsels would make a really elegant present, particularly as they're baked in little paper sweet cases, which gives them a neat, professional look. Our recipe makes enough for about 30 chocolate cups, and although we used chopped ginger throughout, you could easily make some of them with scissor snippings of crystallised pineapple instead. They'll last for up to a month in airtight containers.

Ingredients

175 g (6 oz) of Easy-to-Work Dark plain chocolate (direct or mail order from Baker Smith).
100 g (4 oz) of finely chopped stem or crystallised ginger.

Method

Melt the chocolate in a basin over simmering water. Set out 30 paper sweet cases on a baking sheet or tray. Sprinkle a few pieces of ginger into each of them, and then fill almost to the top with melted chocolate. Finish with more ginger and leave to set.

39 Hazlenut truffles

Easy to make, these aren't as rich as classic truffles, but they still make irresistable eating. Covered in the fridge, they'll keep for up to a week, but let them "come to" at room temperature before devouring. Enough for 25.

Ingredients

125 g (4 oz) of Easy to Work Dark plain chocolate.
50 g (2 oz) of butter.
125 g (4 oz) of trifle sponge cakes.
50 g (2 oz) of icing sugar.
50 g (2 oz) of hazelnuts.
30 ml (2 tablespoonfuls) of brandy.
50 g (2 oz) of chocolate vermicelli.

Method

Brown the hazlenuts under the grill or in the oven, and rub off their skins. Chop them finely and set aside. Put the trifle sponge cakes through a sieve and also set aside.

Melt the chocolate in a basin over simmering water. Cut the butter into small pieces, and stir into the melted chocolate with the sieved sponge cakes and the icing sugar. Beat together well, and then work in the brandy and the chopped hazelnuts. Put the mixture in the fridge until it's firm enough to shape into small balls. It may help to dust your fingers with icing sugar for this task. Finally, roll the balls in chocolate vermicelli until they're coated all over.

40 Marzipan dates

If you can find fresh dates, these petits fours will be even more delicious than usual, and if you wrap them individually in Cling film, they'll keep for up to ten days in the fridge. If you use dried dates they'll be much sweeter, but you'll also find they last rather longer. Enough for about 30.

Ingredients

225 g ($\frac{1}{2}$ lb) of dates.
50 g (2 oz) of icing sugar.
50 g (2 oz) of caster sugar.
175 g (6 oz) of ground almonds.
A small egg white.
15 ml (1 tablespoonful) of lemon juice.
2.5 ml ($\frac{1}{2}$ teaspoonful) of almond essence.

Method

Halve the dates lengthwise, remove the stones and set aside. Sift the icing sugar and caster sugar into a bowl and stir in the ground almonds. Then stir in the lemon juice, the egg white and the almond essence. Work well together, and fill the dates generously with marzipan.

41 Chestnut crackles

These soft marron centres in a crisp toffee coating make a really special treat. They won't keep well for more than a few hours, so unless they're likely to vanish rapidly (our recipe is enough for 30 crackles), you may like to make all the centres in one go, but toffee-coat them in tiny batches. In any case, beginners may find it easier to prepare just half the amount of toffee at a time.

Ingredients

A 275 g (10 oz) can of unsweetened chestnuts.
150 ml ($\frac{1}{4}$ pint) of milk.
75 g (3 oz) of trifle sponge cakes.
275 g (10 oz) of caster sugar.
15 ml (1 tablespoonful) of brandy.
15 ml (1 tablespoonful) of double cream.

Method

Drain the can of chestnuts, put them into a saucepan with the milk, and cook gently for about ten minutes.

Sieve them into a bowl, and then sieve the trifle sponge cakes into the bowl and mix together. Add 50 g (2 oz) of the caster sugar, the brandy and the double cream, and combine all the ingredients. Wet your fingers, and shape the mixture into 30 small balls. Set aside on non-stick paper to form a skin.

Then make as much of the toffee coating as you need. To coat all 30 balls, slowly heat 225 g (8 oz) of the caster sugar in a heavy saucepan, shaking the pan from time to time. When the sugar has dissolved, raise the heat and keep it raised until the melted sugar turns a medium caramel colour. Tip the saucepan to give a depth of toffee, and lower the chestnut balls one at a time on the greased prongs of a fork, or you could use a chocolate dipping fork if you have one. When each marron centre is thinly coated, place it on an oiled plate to set, and when set, sit in paper sweet cases.

PS. These petits fours can also make a spectacular dessert if you place a bowl of cold water on the dining table, rush in the hot crackles straight from the saucepan, and plunge them individually into the water on the prongs of a fork, pulling them out quickly and serving immediately. They will literally crackle—and hiss and spit—just like the toffee apple served in Chinese restaurants.

42 Crème de menthe

This is a classic treat made the simple way. It's very refreshing served at the end of meal.

Ingredients

25 g (1 oz) of powdered gelatine.
300 ml ($\frac{1}{2}$ pint) of cold water.
450 g (1 lb) of granulated sugar.
75 ml (5 tablespoonfuls) of Crème de Menthe liqueur.
A little icing sugar.

Method

Place the powdered gelatine and granulated sugar into a saucepan of the cold water. Heat gently until the sugar has dissolved. Then bring to the boil and continue boiling for about 15 minutes. Remove from the heat and allow to cool slightly, and add the Creme de Menthe liqueur. Pour into a dampened 20.5 cm (8 in) by 15 cm (6 in) cake tin, and leave to set in a cool place for 24 hours. When set, turn out as a slab. Cut into squares and toss in the icing sugar, so it's not sticky to eat and looks cool and frosted.

43 Rum butter

Although traditionally, this is meant to go with Christmas pudding, it's incredibly good with baked apples or poached plums. It's also marvellous spread on hot toast.

If you pack it in small pots and keep it in the fridge, you can help yourself to mere meal-size quantities, so it's always eaten freshly opened.

Ingredients

225 g (8 oz) of unsalted butter.
100 g (4 oz) to 225 g (8 oz) of soft light brown sugar—not demerara.

The grated rind of half a lemon or a small orange.

5 ml (1 teaspoonful) of lemon or orange juice.

45 ml (3 tablespoonfuls) of rum.

Method

Cream the butter and sugar well together until light and fluffy. Beat in the grated lemon or orange rind. Now add the lemon or orange juice and the rum, going drop by drop so the mixture doesn't curdle. Pack into jars.

44 Prunes in brandy

This alcoholic dessert-time treat does wonders for the image of the humble prune. It's an ideal standby for unexpected guests because it will keep until the need arises.

Ingredients

450 g (1 lb) of tendersweet dried prunes.
300 ml ($\frac{1}{2}$ pint) of water.
225 g ($\frac{1}{2}$ lb) of granulated sugar.
150 ml ($\frac{1}{4}$ pint) of brandy.

Method

Simmer the prunes in the water for about ten minutes. Strain the juice, and measure off 300 ml ($\frac{1}{2}$ pint), making the amount up with more water if necessary. Arrange the prunes in smallish jars. Then return the juice to the saucepan and add the granulated sugar. Dissolve the sugar over a low heat and then fast-boil to 110°C (230°F) on a sugar thermometer. Leave to cool, stir in the brandy, pour over the prunes and seal the jars.

45 Spiced apricots

These make a delicious extra to serve with a cold gammon joint or ham, and they look really sumptuous on a buffet table. If you're going to eat them within a week, just place them covered in the fridge, but if you want to keep them longer, or give them away as presents, seal the jars while hot with Porosan skin to ensure good preservation.

Ingredients

A 538 g (1 lb 3 oz) can of apricot halves.
175 g (6 oz) of sugar.
150 ml ($\frac{1}{4}$ pint) of distilled malt vinegar.
8 cloves.
A small stick of cinnamon, broken in half.
4 all-spice berries.

Method

Drain the syrup from the can of apricots, and set it aside. Dissolve the sugar in a saucepan with the vinegar, adding the cloves, the cinnamon and the all-spice berries. Once dissolved, bring to the boil, add the apricot halves, and reduce to a gentle bubble. Leave at this low heat for just five minutes. Then loosely pack the fruit with the spices into heated jars, and fill up with syrup to cover the fruit.

46 Grape mincemeat

Fresh grapes and a few tablespoonfuls of sherry lift traditional mincemeat out of the ordinary. Used in an open-latticed flan liberally sprinkled with blanched almonds, it makes a luscious dessert for all year round, especially served with chilled cream or a small scoop of plain ice-cream.

Ingredients

75 g (3 oz) each of currants, raisins and sultanas.
50 g (2 oz) of chopped mixed peel.
50 g (2 oz) of shredded suet.
150 g (5 oz) of demerara sugar.
5 ml (1 teaspoonful) of ground mixed spice.
The finely grated rind of 1 lemon and 1 orange.
175 g (6 oz) of small green grapes, skinned, halved and pipped.
45 ml (3 tablespoonfuls) of sherry.

Method

Simply mix all the ingredients together and pack densely in any attractive airtight glass or china container.

47

A clever cover story

This elegant floor-length tablecloth cunningly exploits the idea of log cabin patchwork by blowing up just a single cabin. The result is original—and highly economical.

Most large circular tablecloths are expensive to make. To avoid an ugly seam running down the middle, it's necessary to buy three widths of fabric, so the joins can get lost in the folds at the sides. The wastage involved is quite appalling, because less material gets used than gets left over. With this tablecloth, however, there's hardly any waste, and the seams form an integral part of the design.

We used a printed cotton fabric with the mottled look of marble, but you could use any pattern that works well in both directions, or of course, you could simply use plain colours. And although our completed cloth has a 2.8 m (9 ft 4 in) diameter, to cover a standard height table with a 120 cm (48 in) diameter, you could easily adapt it to other sizes.

Materials

- 1 m of 150 cm (59 in) wide Nuage in the red colourway (from Osborne & Little) for the square marked A in the diagram.
- 1.3 m of 150 cm (59 in) wide Nuage in the pink colourway for the strips marked B.
- 2.10 m of 150 cm (59 in) wide Nuage in the yellow colourway for the strips marked C.
- 2.8 m of 150 cm (59 in) wide Nuage in the beige colourway for the strips marked D.

Method

Cut the centre, A, to measure 94 cm (37 in) square. Cut or tear down the length of the fabric four strips, B, to each measure 35.5 cm (14 in) deep by 130 cm (51 in) long. Cut or tear down the length of the fabric four strips, C, to each measure 35.5 cm (14 in) deep by 200 cm (79 in) long. And cut or tear down the length of the fabric four strips, D, to each measure 35.5 cm (14 in) deep by 271 cm ($106\frac{1}{2}$ in) long.

To add the log cabin strips: Leaving 1.25 cm ($\frac{1}{2}$ in) seam allowances throughout, and working with right sides together, machine the first strip of B (B1 in the diagram) along the top of centre square A, so the edges line up at the left. This will leave a 35.5 cm (14 in) overlap of B1 at the top right.

Machine the second strip of B (B2 in the diagram) to the righthand side of centre square A, as shown in Diagram 1, this time leaving a 35.5 cm (14 in) overlap at the bottom right. Then machine the top edge of B2 to the bottom edge of the B1 overlap. Machine the third strip of B (B3 in the diagram) along the bottom of centre square A, to leave a 35.5 cm (14 in) overlap at bottom left. Then machine the righthand edge of B3 to the overlap of B2. Finally, machine the fourth strip of B (B4 in the diagram) to the lefthand side of centre square A, leaving a 35.5 cm (14 in) overlap at the top

left. Then machine the overlap of B4 to the left edge of B1 where you started.

Continue to build up the tablecloth in exactly the same way, adding the strips of C to the strips of B, and the strips of D to the strips of C. It's important always to start work at the top left of the tablecloth, so that, as you proceed, the pattern of seams builds up consistently.

To shape the circle: When you have added all the strips they will form a square, as shown in Diagram 2. Fold the square in half, and then fold it again into a quarter. Use some string, a drawing pin and a pencil, compass-style, to mark out a quarter-circle of the size tablecloth you require. In our case, the string-length measured 142 cm (56 in), and represented half the diameter of the entire cloth. All that remains now is to cut off the surplus corners and hem the tablecloth neatly.

An optional extra: As there is some wastage of fabric D, the beige colour-way, and you will have some scrappy lengths of A, B and C left over, it's possible to make up a set of companion napkins. Cut a 30 cm (12 in) square of D to form the basis of a napkin, and then cut four 41 cm (16 in) long by 10 cm (4 in) deep strips of either fabric A, B or C. The pink colourway, B, forms a particularly attractive contrasting border. Stitch the strips to the centre square of D in exactly the same way as you stitched the first four strips to the tablecloth, only this time, there will only be an overlap of 10 cm (4 in) at each stage. Turn in the raw edges of the strips, and hem neatly to the back of the napkin to conceal the machine stitching. Continue with three more napkins bordered in the same or a different coloured strip.

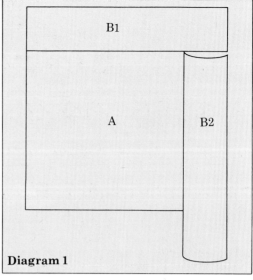

Diagram 1

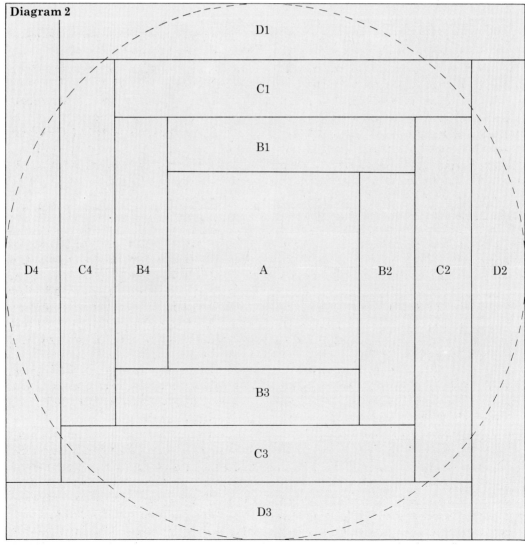

Diagram 2

48

An old-fashioned shell and seaweed picture

Thanks to modern glues, it's easier to tackle traditional shellwork than in the days when each shell needed embedding in plaster. But you still need light and nimble fingers.

In the 18th century, Georgian ladies ornamented picture frames and chandeliers with elegant swags of life-like shell flowers. Their Victorian counterparts carried on the tradition, creating bouquets of shell-flowers to go under glass domes and framing baskets of dried seaweed to hang on the walls. Sadly, few of these domestic treasures survive, so it's just as well that all it takes is a little time and patience, as opposed to special skills, to adapt this enchanting craft for the 20th century. Whether you make no more than a small bouquet, or complete a whole picture, the results will be delectable.

Materials

For the shell-flower bouquets you'll need:

Vari-sized pink shells for the roses (you can find these on most British beaches. Sandy beaches offer the best selection—but don't bother with tarred or rusted shells—they'll be too difficult to clean).

Small white shells for most of the other flowers (mixed packs available direct or mail order from the Eaton Shell Shop).

Any other delicate and petal-like shells that take your fancy.

Some good quality cardboard about the thickness of a shoe-box lid.

Green-covered wire (from craft shops).

Wire cutters (from craft shops—worth buying, or you'll ruin your scissors).

Tweezers (eyebrow-tweezers will do fine—you'll need them for dealing with the smallest and fiddliest shells).

Araldite glue.

For the shell-flower and seaweed picture you'll need:

The same materials as for the bouquets, plus the following:

Feathery seaweeds (you can find these on most British beaches).

A small cane basket (direct or mail order from The Neal Street Shop).

A craft knife (from craft or art shops).

A thin card mount.

A tube of Uhu glue.

Method

Scrub shells found on the beach in warm soapy water and leave to dry. Sort all shells into groups according to colour, size and "direction". The shells used for the roses come naturally in pairs: it's important to use one set of halves for one flower and the other for another.

It's also important to use the larger, paler shells for the outside petals, and the smaller, deeper-shaded shells for the central petals.

Cut out circles of cardboard using 1p and 2p pieces as guides. Pierce the centre of the circles with a thick darning needle. Cut off a piece of wire about 20 cm (8 in) long and, working from the underside of the circle, push one end up through the hole in the centre and secure the wire to the card by bending it over the edge and bringing it back to the centre underneath.

Have ready a large cardboard box pierced with holes, so that as you complete each flower, you can push its wire stem through a hole, and give the flower-head support until the Araldite has set. As this will take at least 24 hours, be sure to put the box where it won't be disturbed.

To make the single daisies: Start with the simple, single-layered daisies, and then progress to the roses which are trickier to handle. Choosing smaller shells for a 1p-size circle or larger shells for a 2p-size circle, cover the top of a cardboard base with a thick layer of Araldite. Stick the first shell next to where the wire crosses over, so the side of the shell overlaps it. (This way you don't risk sticking a petal on top of the wire, which would make it project from the others.) Stick on the remaining shells so that each overlaps the other slightly, working in a clockwise direction, and easing in the shells as near to the centre as possible. If you cannot avoid a gap in the centre, fill it with a tiny shell or pearl.

To make the double roses: Cover the top of a cardboard base with Araldite. Starting on the perimeter of the circle, next to the wire, arrange a layer of the largest shells, each overlapping the other slightly, in a clockwise direction as near to the edge as possible. As you stick, tilt the shells to give a cupped effect. Stick another layer of the smaller, more deeply coloured shells inside the first, in the same way, and complete with two or three of the smaller shells in the centre. At this stage, you can shape the flower with your fingertips if needed.

All the flowers are made on exactly the same principle, using petals and cardboard bases of different sizes to give larger or smaller blooms. When the flowers are dry, paint the back of the bases green to match the stems.

For a bouquet, just arrange in any sympathetic container—cutting or doubling up the wire stems to give varying flower heights.

Preparing the seaweed: For the picture, prepare the feathery seaweed by rinsing it well to get rid of any sand. Best way is to fill the kitchen sink with water and let each piece float on the surface. To retain its filigree form, slide a sheet of writing paper under each piece of seaweed and lift out of the water. This way the fronds arrange themselves naturally on the paper. Place the wet sheets of paper on the sides of the bath to dry, and after a day or two, the seaweed can be carefully peeled from its paper backing.

Finding the frame: Unless you are going to have one specially made, the next essential is to find the picture frame—because this will determine the size of your mount and how you arrange everything on the mount. It will need to have enough depth between its back and the glass to accommodate the three-dimensional flowers, so look either for a deep-sided box-frame, or a frame with convex glass such as we used. Ours happens to be a genuine Victorian example, and you should be able to find something similar if you scour antique and junk shops. Its circular frame dictated a circular arrangement—you would need to reinterpret the arrangement for a square or rectangular frame.

Once found, cut the thin card to the appropriate size. Then, using your craft knife, slice a shallow section from the small cane basket. Fix the section of the basket to the card with a few stitches of strong matching thread, tying the ends securely at the back. Arrange the fronds of seaweed and shell flowers in the basket, snipping wire stems and bending flower heads as necessary. When you're happy with the positioning of this "dry run", stick everything down on the mount securely using the Uhu adhesive.

49

A snappy box of crackers

Shop-bought crackers can be disappointing. If you're tired of plastic charms and threadbare mottos, why not make your own and be sure of the contents?

Christmas crackers are a true-blue British invention, even if the London sweetshop owner who dreamt them up was inspired by the elegant shape of French bonbons. Quite why he added a "crack" and a paper hat, plus a love message rather than a joke or motto, is shrouded in the mists of time. But Victorians took to them with enthusiasm, and when they made their own at home, they decorated them with frills, scrap pictures and artificial flowers.

Today most crackers are made from crinkly crêpe paper because it moulds into a cracker shape obediently. But that doesn't mean you can't use anything else. You could make dazzling crackers from shiny kitchen foil, and any thinnish sheets of paper will do.

These crackers were made from wrapping papers, and as there are literally hundreds to choose from in the shops, the creative scope is virtually unlimited. If you wanted to get away from the conventional Christmassy look, you could choose a plain, dull-gold wrapping paper, and decorate it with cut-outs from a shiny gold doily.

We decided to keep to traditional colours and hunted for papers in bright red and green, but we chose distinctly untraditional patterns, like polka dots and tiny all-over flowers. Two of the papers were double-faced, with related patterns on front and back, which means some of our crackers look as good inside as out. You do catch a

glimpse of the insides as you pull a cracker, but this refinement's for fun —it's not an essential.

Actually making the crackers is not too tricky. You need a pair of "formers" to shape the cracker, and although you could use a cardboard tube cut in two (if so, it'll need a 4 cm ($1\frac{1}{2}$ in) diameter, and you'll need to cut one 23 cm (9 in) and one 13 cm ($5\frac{1}{8}$ in) length) you'll get more professional results with proper aluminium-tube formers. As these are not expensive to buy, they're certainly worth the investment if you intend to make your own crackers every year. The size of formers we recommend you make or buy will produce a 25 cm (10 in) long cracker, and all our measurements are based on this recommendation.

Materials

A pair of size 5 formers (from The Stoneleigh Mail Order Company).
A 30 cm (12 in) by 18 cm (7 in) piece of wrapping paper. If using crêpe, make sure the grain runs lengthways.
A 15 cm (6 in) by 9 cm ($3\frac{1}{2}$ in) piece of card, for stiffening.
A "crack" (from the Stoneleigh Mail Order Company).
A small gift and motto (also available from the Stoneleigh).
A length of string.
A tube of Uhu glue.
Some holly berries or red cherries (from stationers around Christmas).

Method

Place the wrapping paper right side down on a flat surface, such as a table. Referring to Diagram 1, position the "crack" and motto, with card stiffener on top, and the two formers on top of the card. (If you're using crêpe paper, add a 28 cm (11 in) by 15 cm (6 in) piece of lining paper first.)

Dab the top edge of the wrapping paper with glue, and rolling away from you, roll up the paper tightly over the formers. Hold until glue adheres.

To make the first "neck": Gently ease out the shorter, righthand former by about 1.25 cm ($\frac{1}{2}$ in), as shown in Diagram 2. Try not to let the former slip out altogether, as it's hard to replace. Tie the string to a far leg of the table. Pass the string over the part of the cracker with the 1.25 cm ($\frac{1}{2}$ in) gap left by sliding out the former, and loop it round once.

Making sure the cracker is at right angles to the string, pull the string tightly to form a closed "neck". Unwind the string, slip the shorter former back in, and twist it slightly to give a crisp edge. Then pull the shorter former out altogether.

To pop in the gift: Carefully ease out the longer, lefthand former until it's just clear of the stiffening card and about 2.5 cm (1 in) beyond it. Pick up the cracker, supporting the former so it doesn't fall out, and drop the gift into the end of the former. Make sure it drops right through to the already formed "neck".

To make the second neck: Turn the cracker round as shown in Diagram C, so the former is now on the righthand side. Pass the string over the gap left by sliding out the remaining former, and loop it round once, just as you did when you were making the first "neck". This time, however, only pull the string lightly to make a slight impression. Then loop the string round a second time and pull tightly. Unwind the string, slip the former back in, give a slight twist, and pull it out.

To decorate the cracker: This is very much a matter of individual taste. You could simply tie a ribbon round the middle with a bow; you could stick on cut-out paper shapes. For personal gifts, just tie on the relevant name tag.

As these crackers were made from mix-and-match papers, it made sense to continue the co-ordinated theme, adding leaf decorations made from the same papers, and mixing and matching the patterns still further.

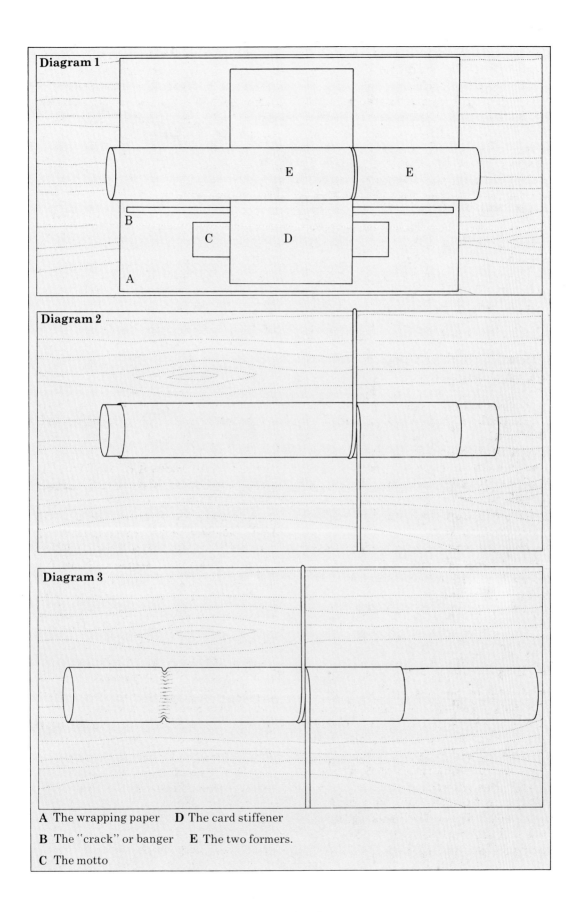

Diagram 1

E   E

B

C   D

A

Diagram 2

Diagram 3

A The wrapping paper   **D** The card stiffener

B The "crack" or banger   **E** The two formers.

C The motto

50

A dramatic duvet cover

Most duvet covers come in pretty florals—but not everyone wants a feminine bedroom. For those who hanker after something more crisp and original, here's a highly striking alternative.

If you could find a duvet cover like this in a shop, you can be sure it would boast a strikingly high price-tag. For some reason, anything that's deliberately design-conscious, particularly if it comes in bright, primary colours, provokes a truly dramatic mark-up. The only way round this financial stumbling block is to make something bright and design-conscious yourself. Our cover, with geometric patches of colour on plain white sheeting, emphatically framed in bold black ribbon, was inspired by Mondrian's abstract paintings. There are ribbon-framed pillowcases to match.

Materials

Duvet cover 4.10 m of white polyester/cotton sheeting, 228 cm (90 in) wide. This is enough to make a 200 cm (79 in) square cover, suitable for a standard double-size bed.
1.4 m of red polyester/cotton fabric, 112 cm (44 in) wide.
1.4 m of yellow polyester/cotton fabric, 112 cm (44 in) wide.
25 cm of blue polyester/cotton fabric, 112 cm (44 in) wide.
8.5 m of black taffeta ribbon, 5 cm (2 in) wide.
2.1 m of poppertape.
  (All available from John Lewis and branches of the John Lewis Partnership.)
Pillowcases 1.7 m of white polyester/cotton fabric, 112 cm (44 in) wide.

This is enough to make a pair of 75 cm ($29\frac{1}{2}$ in) by 50 cm ($19\frac{1}{2}$ in) pillowcases.
4.9 m of black taffeta ribbon, 5 cm (2 in) wide.
  (Again, all available from John Lewis etc.)

Method

Because the design depends for its appeal on the contrast of its vertical and horizontal lines, it's important they read "true". To this end, we suggest washing all the fabrics (including the black ribbon) first. We also suggest tearing the fabric along the grain rather than cutting it. If the torn fabric doesn't seem straight, it can always be slightly dampened and pulled into shape. *N.B.* The cover can be used any way round—there's no such thing as a top or bottom. In fact, in terms of the directions below, our photograph shows the cover "upside down".

To make the top of the duvet cover: Tear two shapes measuring 203 cm (80 in) by 202 cm ($79\frac{1}{2}$ in) from the white sheeting. On each piece, mark one of the longer sides with a pin. Then from the red fabric, tear a piece 133 cm ($52\frac{1}{4}$ in) by 27 cm ($10\frac{5}{8}$ in); from the blue, a piece 48 cm (19 in) by 23 cm (9 in); and from the yellow, a piece 128 cm ($50\frac{1}{2}$ in) by 23 cm (9 in). Iron all the pieces. Spread one large piece of white sheeting on the floor. The pin indicates the top and right side.

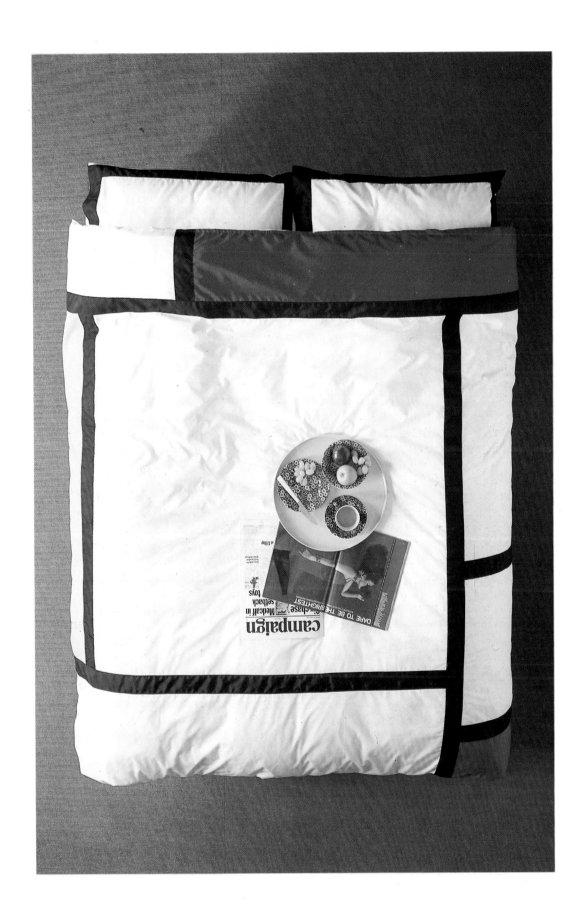

Place the blue patch in the top, left-hand corner of the piece of white sheeting, long side along the top, with raw edges together. Then place the red patch in the bottom left corner, long side along the bottom, with the left edge 5 cm (2 in) in from the edge of the white. Position the yellow long edge against the right edge 45 cm ($17\frac{3}{4}$ in) down from the top. Tack the three patches to the piece of white sheeting.

Cut a 128 cm ($50\frac{1}{2}$ in) length of black taffeta ribbon and pin it along the left hand side of the yellow patch so the ribbon overlaps the patch by 1.5 cm ($\frac{5}{8}$ in). With black thread, machine the ribbon close to each edge. Cut a 153 cm (60 in) length of black ribbon. Starting at a point on the right edge, 41.5 cm ($16\frac{3}{8}$ in) from the top, lay the ribbon so it overlaps the top of the yellow by 1.5 cm ($\frac{5}{8}$ in) and falls short of the left edge by 50 cm ($19\frac{1}{2}$ in). Next cut two 27 cm ($10\frac{5}{8}$ in) lengths of ribbon and pin one on the right edge of the red, overlapping it by 1.5 cm ($\frac{5}{8}$ in). Pin the other piece at the left end of the red, overlapping it by the same amount, so the left edge of the ribbon is just under 1.5 cm ($\frac{5}{8}$ in) from the left edge of the white. Machine both in place.

Cut two 48 cm ($18\frac{7}{8}$ in) lengths of black ribbon. Pin the first length 21.5 cm ($8\frac{1}{2}$ in) down from the top along the edge of the blue. Again starting from the left, pin the second length 76.5 cm (30 in) down from the top to run parallel with the previous length of ribbon. Machine both in place.

Cut a 173 cm (68 in) length of black ribbon. Starting at the top, pin it 46.5 cm ($18\frac{3}{8}$ in) in from the left edge so that it overlaps the right edge of the blue. Machine in place.

Cut a 203 cm (80 in) length of ribbon and pin it across the whole width of the white, 25 cm (10 in) above the bottom, so that it overlaps the top of the red patch. Machine the ribbon into place. Then, using a warm iron, press the whole piece carefully.

To make up the duvet cover: Turn the bottom edge of the completed duvet-top under 5 mm ($\frac{3}{16}$ in) to the wrong side and tack. Using a zipper foot, machine a band of poppertape close to the folded edge to cover the tacked edge. On the remaining piece of white sheeting, turn the edge marked with a pin under 5 mm ($\frac{3}{16}$ in) and tack. Machine a second band of poppertape so that it corresponds to the first band on the duvet top.

With right sides of the duvet top and the duvet bottom together, machine the sides and top 1.5 cm ($\frac{5}{8}$ in) from the raw edge. Trim the seam to 6 mm ($\frac{1}{4}$ in) and zig-zag together. Turn the cover right side up and iron.

To make the matching pillowcases: Tear two rectangles 163 cm (64 in) by 53 cm ($20\frac{7}{8}$ in) from white fabric. Turn a 3 cm ($1\frac{1}{4}$ in) hem along one short side and tack. This makes your right side.

Cut two 69 cm ($27\frac{1}{8}$ in) lengths of black ribbon, and lay the fabric on a table, right side up, with the tacked edge to the right. Pin one length of ribbon 1.5 cm ($\frac{5}{8}$ in) below the top edge, starting from the edge of the right hem. Machine in place. Pin the second length of ribbon 1.5 cm ($\frac{5}{8}$ in) above the bottom edge, starting from the right hem. Machine in place.

Cut two 53 cm ($20\frac{7}{8}$ in) lengths of ribbon. Pin the first length along the right edge, just covering it so that no white shows. Machine in place. Pin the second length across the pillowcase, with its left edge 75 cm ($29\frac{1}{2}$ in) from the right edge of the pillowcase. Machine in place. On the remaining short edge, turn under 6 mm ($\frac{1}{4}$ in) to the wrong side and machine. Make a 10 cm (4 in) turning to the wrong side and tack. With right sides together, fold the fabric in half, with the machined ends together.

Machine the long sides together at top and bottom. Trim the seams to 6 mm ($\frac{1}{4}$ in) and zig-zag together. Turn to the right sides and press.

Where to find everything

Throughout this book, we've tried to suggest stockists who not only sell direct, but through the post too. Here we give their addresses (in alphabetical order), plus any further information that might prove useful. We also include stockists not previously mentioned—either because they're in different areas, which increases the chance of your being able to buy locally—or because they have such a good specialist range, that they're worth knowing about.

In some cases, comprehensive mail-order catalogues are available; in others only a descriptive price list; whilst others will simply reply by letter if you write with a specific query. As for possible charges, they're similarly variable. Some mail-order catalogues are free, others are not —particularly if they include actual samples. Some cost money which is refundable if you order a certain amount. There may, in any case, be a minimum order requirement.

As prices and policies are always subject to change, rather than give information that could quickly date, we suggest you write to individual stockists for mail-order details. *Remember, of course, to send a stamped addressed envelope.*

Although most of the beautiful things in this book require no special expertise to make, they may inspire you to more ambitious projects, so we suggest a few helpful leaflets and books. And as many of them need sticking rather than stitching, we give a brief guide on the glues. You'll find everything even simpler if you use the right ones.

**Afrasian Imports,
2 Kneesworth Street,
Royston,
Hertfordshire SG8 0NN.**
This company sells by mail order only, so not surprisingly, they have a comprehensive catalogue. As well as large, exotic **shells**, you can buy packets of smaller mixed shells; but even smaller ones—ideal for the shell and seaweed picture (*No 48*)—are sold by the no-nonsense pound. (See also under The Tropical Shells Company and The Eaton Shell Shop.)

**Baker Smith,
65 The Street,
Tongham,
Farnham,
Surrey GU10 1DE.**
Baker Smith's is a school of **cake decorating**, but it supplies to the public direct and mail order. There's no catalogue, but the price list is self-explanatory. It includes edible decorations like little flowers; piped icing equipment for ribbons and scrolls; cake stands and pillars for wedding cakes.

**Berisfords Ltd,
PO Box 2,
Congleton,
Cheshire CW12 1EF.**
This company boasts an astounding array of mouth-watering ribbons and trimmings. We used their trimmings for some of the pillowcases (No 1); also used their satin bias binding for the scalloped towels (No 33). Ribbons come in satin, taffeta and velvet, plus prints and fancy weaves, including organdies, picot, checks and tartans.

There are plain or ruched broderie anglais edgings, ribbon-threaded lace trimmings, macramés, and all manner of braids, pipings, cords and knitted and string sequin trimmings.

Only available through stockists, who should have free copies of Berisfords' Ribbon News leaflets. If not, they'll be sent, on receipt of a stamped addressed envelope, from: Dean Crest Publicity, Howey Hill, Congleton, Cheshire CW12 4AF. (See also under C. M. Offray & Sons Ltd.)

Candle Maker Supplies,
28 Blythe Road,
London W14.

This shop sells everything needed for **candlemaking**, from wax, wicks and dyes to dipping cans and thermometers. To give some idea of their comprehensive stock, they offer over 150 different moulds. Their booklet, Making Candles, is a cheap step-by-step guide that tells beginners all the essentials, but they also sell video cassettes on the subject, and hold reasonably priced candlemaking classes. A mail-order catalogue is available.

Most craft shops and big department stores sell candlemaking equipment. As this usually comes from Candle Maker Supplies in the first place, you can write to them for stockists.

Combined Optical Industries Ltd,
Slough,
Buckinghamshire.

Really close work can prove tiring to the eyes. We're thinking of the embroidered jug of nasturtiums (*No 31*) and the cat on the mat tapestry (*No 26*). So it could be worth investing in an **Easy-View magnifying glass**. This comes with an adjustable cord for hanging round the neck, and with a frame that rests on the chest or stomach, leaving hands free to work.

If you can't find it in the haberdashery department of your local store, or your local needlework shop, it's available direct or mail order from The Danish House; or mail order only from the makers, Combined Opticals.

Creative Beadcraft Ltd,
Unit 26,
Chiltern Trading Estate,
Earl Howe Road,
Holmer Green,
High Wycombe,
Buckinghamshire HP15 6QT.

Creative Beadcraft is the mail-order arm of Ells & Farrier, and stocks its entire range of **beads, sequins, imitation stones and trimmings**. The mail order catalogue is stiff with actual samples that make you rack your brains for ways of using them.

Culpeper Ltd,
Hadstock Road,
Linton,
Cambridgeshire CB1 6NJ
(mail order only).

Culpeper Ltd,
9 Flask Walk,
London NW3.

Culpeper Ltd,
21 Bruton Street,
London W1.

Culpeper Ltd,
8 The Market,
Covent Garden,
London WC2
(direct shoppers only).

Other shops at Bath, Brighton, Cambridge, Guildford, Norwich, Oxford, Salisbury and Winchester.

Culpeper sell ready-made **pot pourris and sleep herbs**, as well as the **essential oils, fixatives and spices** needed for making your own. They also sell a blend of essential oils for reviving existing pot pourris.

All available direct or mail order, as is their helpful booklet, Making Your Own Pot Pourri, which includes a selection of recipes. (See also under The Herb Society; Meadow Herbs; John Bell & Croyden.)

The Danish House,
16 Sloane Street,
London SW1

The Danish House specialises in **counted cross-stitch needlework**, but is London's best source of **general embroidery materials** too, which makes it well worth a visit from personal shoppers.

Although they will supply individual mail-order catalogues, it's cheaper to register for their full catalogue list —but only if you're interested in cross-stitch work, as this is what most of them deal with exclusively.

The Eaton Shell Shop
16 Manette Street,
London W1.

Although they have many exotic **shells**, and stock rare items for serious collectors, they also sell packs of small mixed shells—suitable for the shell and seaweed picture (*No 48*).

They supply direct or mail order. (See also under Afrasian Imports; and The Tropical Shells Company Ltd.)

Egg Elegance,
30 Red House Lane,
Bexleyheath,
Kent DA6 8JD.

Decorating Easter eggs can be a matter of simple fun (*No 11*), or it can be a complicated Fabergé-type art. Whole books get devoted to the subject, and they're available, along with an astonishing array of materials, by mail order from these suppliers.

For intricately painted eggs, Egg Elegance sell intermixable acrylic paints and ceramic paints which come in very rich colours, plus suitable clear varnishes to protect them. Achievable effects can vary from patchwork and abstract, to lovely peasant motifs.

And for people who lack the confidence to paint free-hand, they sell a very wide selection of transfers. These range from flowers, birds, butterflies and miniature country landscapes, to religious subjects and "Gainsborough" ladies. Once applied, all they need is a coat of clear varnish.

But decorating the eggs can be just a beginning. Although we personally feel it's best to stop there, Egg Elegance also supply the following: a range of finials to decorate the tops of eggs; hinges, for eggs that have been cut in half, and either painted inside or lined with fabric; filigree shapes for eggs that have been given "windows"; all manner of gilt and silver braids; and elaborate stands to hold the completed article—everything from a three-legged lion's paw to a cupid pushing a wheelbarrow.

PS on eggs. If you want to serve coloured eggs on Easter morning, add a dye to the water you boil them in. This will only colour the shell—not the egg-white itself. McCormick's intermixable food colours come in red, green, blue and yellow, and are available from most good grocers and supermarkets. Just follow the instructions on the packet for quantities, adding vinegar to the boiling water before adding the food colour, drop by drop. A three-minute egg will turn a pretty but pale shade; a hard-boiled egg, a gloriously deep colour.

Ells & Farrier,
5 Princes Street,
Hanover Square,
London W1.

This tiny shop, known as The Bead House, is an Aladdin's Cave of glittering treasure. It's full of **beads, sequins, imitation stones and trimmings**—about 340 types in all, although when they're multiplied by the number of colours available, there's a choice of 1,800. The selection of sequins is especially good. Ells & Farrier only sell direct, but their entire range comes mail order from Creative Beadcraft Ltd. (See also under The Hobby Horse.)

The Felt & Hessian Shop,
34 Greville Street,
London EC1.
This shop has the best range of **felts** in the country. They come in 77 colours, 182 cm (72 in) wide, and in three different weights. Superfine Felt would be best for backing the butterfly and flower cushions (*No 6*)—and also ideal for making "instant" curtains. Hessian comes in the same width but in 43 colours. If you're interested in making smaller items, their bundles of felt or hessian off-cuts are a real bargain. These are sold by the weight in assorted colours.

There's no mail-order catalogue as such, but you can write for details of their sample cards, which give all the colours in the range.

John Lewis and John Lewis Partnership shops also sell felt by the metre, 36 in (90 cm) wide, in 25 colours. But craft shops only tend to supply it in small pre-cut squares for toy-making.

Fred Aldous,
The Handicraft Centre,
PO Box 135,
37 Lever Street,
Manchester M60 1UX.
A shop that maintains an enormous stock—there's hardly an art or craft that's not covered, from stained glass, lace-making and leatherwork to marquetry, basketry and pewter work. It keeps a very wide selection of macramé threads. You could browse round the premises—or mail-order catalogue —for weeks. If you would like to know more about the technique of macramé, the following leaflets from Fred Aldous deal with the subject: 906 Beginners; S2501 For Every Purse; 843 Inside-Outside; 819 Home Decor. A book called *Macramé Start*, HP193, is also available. Fred Aldous maintains a comprehensive stock of patchwork templates too, including $\frac{3}{8}$ in (1 cm) and $\frac{1}{2}$ in (1.2 cm) hexagon window templates.

Glorafilia,
The Old Mill House,
The Ridgeway,
Mill Hill Village,
London NW7.
A shop that sells the entire range of handpainted and screen printed Glorafilia **tapestry kits**, renowned for their quality and style. It also sells, direct or mail order, everything needed for all kinds of tapestry. A catalogue is available: it's a source of inspiration to both beginners and experts.

The Handicraft Shop,
47 Northgate,
Canterbury,
Kent CT1 1BA.
One of the few reliable sources of the traditional **wooden clothes pegs** needed for the dolls (*No 30*). They sell direct or mail order, and cater for a stimulating range of handicrafts, including **basketry, candlemaking, collage, crochet, flowermaking, lacemaking, leatherwork, macramé, patchwork and tapestry.** Their illustrated catalogue makes fascinating reading. Your local craft shop may stock wooden two-prong pegs; so might an old-fashioned ironmonger if you can find one.

The Herb Society,
34 Boscobel Place,
London SW1.
You don't have to belong to the society to buy the fascinating booklets they publish. The titles give a clear indication of their contents: Herbal Hair Colouring; A Guide to **Spices**; and Growing **Herbs**.

If you want to make an old-fashioned pomander of sweet smelling beads, for wearing as a bracelet or necklace, *Pomanders, Washballs and other Scented Articles* is the relevant booklet. Washballs turn out to be recipes for soap, and other scented articles include scent bags and several different types of pot pourri.

The Hobby Horse Ltd,
15–17 Langton Street,
London SW10.
The Hobby Horse probably has the largest selection of **beads** in the country. They're imported direct from all over the world and include handmade Venetian glass beads, hand-painted Indian glass beads, solid brass, bone, seed and plastic beads. But their semi-precious beads are perhaps the most covetable. These come in everything from jade, agate, coral and amethyst to rose quartz, tiger eye, malachite and turquoise.

Because they're mainly for people with jewellery in mind, the Hobby Horse also specialises in jewellery "findings" like earring clips and necklace clasps. Their range of sequins is very good too; they even stock the brass bell needed for the cat on the mat tapestry (*No 26*). All supplied direct or mail order, and a comprehensive colour catalogue is available.

John Bell & Croyden,
54 Wigmore Street,
London W1.
This specialist chemist shop sells natural essential oils for making sleep herbs and pot pourri, and a range of synthetic essential oils. These are much cheaper than the natural kind, and it takes a very discerning nose to tell the difference. Sold direct or mail order, when a stock list is available.

John Lewis,
Oxford Street,
London W1.
John Lewis Partnership shops in the London area:
Peter Jones,
    Sloane Square,
    London SW1.
Jones Brothers,
    Holloway Road,
    London N7.
John Lewis,
    Brent Cross Shopping Centre,
London NW4.
Pratts,
    Streatham High Road,
    London SW16.
John Lewis Partnership shops throughout the country:
John Lewis,
    The Horsefair,
    Bristol BF1 3LF.
Robert Sayle,
    St Andrew's Street,
    Cambridge CB2 3DL.
John Lewis,
    St James' Centre,
    Edinburgh EH1 3FP.
George Henry Lee,
    Basnett Street,
    Liverpool L1 1EA.
John Lewis,
    Central Milton Keynes,
    Milton Keynes MK9 3EP.
Bainbridge,
    Eldon Square,
    Newcastle-upon-Tyne, NE99 1AD.
Jessop & Son,
    Victoria Centre,
    Nottingham NG1 3QA.
John Lewis,
    Queensgate Centre,
    Peterborough, TE1 1NL.
Heelas,
    Broad Street,
    Reading RG1 2BB.
Cole Brothers,
    Barkers Pool,
    Sheffield S1 1ET.
Tyrrell & Green,
    Above Bar,
    Southampton SO9 5HU.
Knight & Lee,
    Palmerston Road,
    Southsea PO5 3QE.
Trewin Brothers,
    Queens Road,
    Watford WD1 2LQ.
Caleys,
    High Street,
    Windsor SL4 1LL.

The John Lewis Partnership offers an excellent range of good quality and reasonably priced materials. This is why we have quoted it as a stockist so often. Its **haberdashery** departments are unsurpassed for their wide selection of ribbons and trimmings etc. And its fabric departments, both furnishing and dressmaking, include materials made by the Partnership itself, which have no equivalent elsewhere.

The **polyester/cotton sheeting**, for instance, which we suggest for the duvet cover (*No 50*), comes in strong, primary colours that are unavailable from any other source. (Although see under Limericks for different-coloured deep dyed sheeting.) The cotton terry towelling, used for the scalloped and satin bound towels (*No 33*), is the only towelling that comes in really subtle and exciting colours. There are about thirty shades in all to choose from.

In fact, with very few exceptions, if you can get to any of the John Lewis Partnership shops, you can get the materials needed for our beautiful things. They stock everything from shells to candle-making kits, and they also deliver or send through the post.

Limericks (Linens) Ltd,
Limerick House,
117 Victoria Avenue,
Southend-on-Sea,
Essex SS2 6EL.
Limericks supply goods mail order only, and produce a comprehensive colour-printed catalogue. One of its main strengths lies in the range of **sheeting**. All-cotton sheeting comes in white, beige, pink, blue, primrose, lilac and green. Polyester/cotton sheeting comes in pastels like pink, blue, primrose, light coffee and white, but also in some sophisticated deep-dyed colours like French blue, green, brown and wine. Several other types of sheeting are available, as well as sometimes hard-to-find fabrics like butter muslin, cheesecloth, cambric, cream embroidery linen, fine white Irish linen and cotton damask.

Limericks also supply 90 cm (36 in) wide cotton/viscose **terry towelling** by the metre, in pink, sky blue, russet, royal blue, green, lemon, daffodil, beige, lovat and white. This could be suitable for the scalloped and satin bound towels (*No 33*), although we preferred the colour range and all-cotton quality of John Lewis's terry towelling.

R. V. Marriner,
Knowle Mills,
South Street,
Keighley,
West Yorkshire BD21 1DW.
(Please mark mail-order requests for the attention of E. H. Williamson.)
Marriner Choice **Aran pure wool** is also available direct or mail order from The Knitters World, 263–271, Holloway Road, London, N7.

Meadow Herbs,
39 Moreton Street,
London SW1
(Direct shoppers only).

Meadow Herbs,
Copthall Place,
Anna Valley,
Andover,
Hampshire
(Mail order only).
Meadow Herbs sell **sleep herbs** ready-spiced and oiled; they also sell **spices, essential oils and fixatives**, for making your own sleep herbs or pot pourri. Their complete pot pourri kits are particularly attractive: these pack everything you need except the flowers and petals into a miniature chest of drawers.

Other merchandise includes booklets on herbs and pot pourri; hops; seven types of ready-made pot pourri; and a "booster" blend of essential oils for revitalising an existing pot pourri. This can be a real money saver. (See also under Culpeper and The Herb Society.)

The Neal Street Shop,
23 and 29 Neal Street,
London WC2.
This is a gift shop specialising in Chinese items, and it always has an excellent range of **cane and wicker bowls and baskets**. Even so, stocks of the miniature size holding the pomander (*No 2*) cannot be guaranteed. The Neal Street Shops supply by post but there's no mail-order catalogue—it's a matter of writing and asking for details.

Branches of Habitat throughout the country also stock a very good range. It never appears in their mail-order catalogue and is only available to direct shoppers, because supplies from third world countries are irregular.

Department stores frequently have good selections too, but again, supplies fluctuate and can't be relied on. If you're stumped for a local stockist, you could try your nearest florist—or even a jumble sale. And it's amazing the uses to which you can put attractive jars and old chianti baskets!

C. M. Offray & Sons Ltd,
Fir Tree Place,
Church Road,
Ashford,
Middlesex TW15 2PH.
Most of the ribbons used in this book were made by Offray, whose range is so enormous, shops can only stock a selection. Although Offray do not sell mail order, it's still worth writing for details of their catalogue, because then you can ask shops to order a particular ribbon, or write to Offray for your nearest stockist.

Any shops selling Offray ribbons should, in theory, have a supply of free Offray leaflets. These are full of good ideas plus how-to instructions, and subjects covered include ribbon weaving, making ribbon roses, and making satin flowers for bridal head-wreaths. (See also under Ries Wools of Holborn and Berisfords Ltd.)

Osborne & Little,
304 Kings Road,
London SW3.
This shop is an excellent source of small patterned **wallpapers and matching materials**, which are sophisticated rather than fussily pretty. Most good decorating shops throughout the country supply their ranges.

Paperchase,
216 Tottenham Court Road,
London W1.

Paperchase,
167 Fulham Road,
London SW3.
Perfectionists, who pay as much care to wrapping presents as finding them in the first place, will risk overspending in either of these shops.

It's very hard to resist their **wrapping papers** (including some with reversible patterns); their ribbons; little marbleised boxes; delectable labels; and endless etceteras that you can't find elsewhere. They also stock a discerning range of craft books—vetting out the velvet-covered tissue-dispenser variety. A mail-order catalogue is available, but for the papers and art materials only.

The Patchwork Dog and
Calico Cat Ltd,
21 Chalk Farm Road,
London NW1.
This shop has virtually **everything for the patchwork addict**, from all conceivable types of template, including strip templates for log cabin designs. Also very useful is their Hexagon Polygrid—a sheet of clear plastic marked with seven different-sized hexagons, from 12.5 mm ($\frac{1}{2}$ in) upwards. Other Polygrids offer seven sizes of diamonds, pointed diamonds, squares and right-angled triangles.

The Patchwork Dog stocks over 500 small-print fabrics; sells a selection of antique patchworks; and also sells everything needed for quilting. Write for details of their mail-order catalogue, and if interested, for dates of the patchwork courses they run.

Most craft shops also sell hexagon templates, although the 9.5 mm ($\frac{3}{8}$ in) size may be hard to find. (However, see under Fred Aldous for a reliable source.) They may, like The Patchwork Dog, stock Colers Patch Plates. These are template packs with sewing instructions on the back, and therefore very useful for beginners. Hexagon sizes begin at 12.5 mm ($\frac{1}{2}$ in).

For advanced patchwork enthusiasts, *Good Housekeeping Patchwork and Appliqué,* published by Ebury Press, with 96 colour pages and full instructions, is recommended reading. Also recommended: *Good Housekeeping Crochet,* which is part of the same series. It's ideal for both beginners and experienced crochet hands.

Ries Wools of Holborn,
**242–243 High Holborn,
London WC1.**

Ries Wools of Hackney,
**42 Clarence Road,
London E5.**
Ries are one of Offray Ribbons', major London stockists, and they will supply by post as well as direct. (See also under C. M. Offray & Sons Ltd.) As their name suggests, they sell mainly **wools**, and keep a wide range of most good quality brands—including the Patons wools needed for the butterfly and flower cushions (*No 6*). But they're also strong on haberdashery and anything connected with tapestry.

Russell & Chapple Ltd,
**23 Monmouth Street,
London WC2.**
A marvellous source of all kinds of **canvases, hessians, linens, jute and cotton twills**—mostly available in varying widths. They have too vast a range for a mail-order catalogue, but if you write explaining your requirements (they're very knowledgeable about what's best for which situation), they'll send relevant samples.

Stoneleigh Mail Order Company,
**91 Prince Avenue,
Southend-on Sea,
Essex.**
A company that offers all possible **cracker-making ingredients**—from the formers and ready-cut papers, to the "cracks", mottos and fillings. Mail-order catalogue available. Also a price list for carnival supplies—an inspirational source of joke items, from scabs ("really horrible" claims the blurb) to raspberry blowers ("rude noise") and squashed rats ("yu-ukk").

The Tropical Shells Company Ltd,
**22 Preston Road,
Brighton,
Sussex BN1 4QF.**
This shop sells direct and mail order. They make up "standard" and "quantity" packs for craftwork, and these are what you need for the shell and seaweed picture (*No 48*). Most of their other **shells** are too large—or rare—for the purpose.

Appendix notes
Glues.
Although there are dozens of glues on the market (each manufacturer offers a range of specific glues for specific jobs), in practice you could make all the beautiful things in this book using only two different types—a laytex adhesive like Copydex or Bostik 11 and an all-purpose clear adhesive like Uhu or Bostik 1.

Laytex adhesives are ideal for sticking soft materials like paper, fabric and leather; clear adhesives better for hard materials like wood, pottery, metal and shells. Whichever you use, the main thing is to read the instructions first—not turn to them when all else has failed.

Acknowledgements

All the designs throughout this book were specially commissioned by **Diana Austen**, Homes Editor of Good Housekeeping. Its success is due to her sure judgement. She has an unerring eye for the true and beautiful—and will never settle for anything less.

Diana and the author would like to thank the following designers for their contributions:

Pat Barnett, who designed the paper-patchwork screen (*No 4*); the flower and butterfly cushions (*No 6*); the crocheted flower picture (*No 24*); the dried flower bouquet in a basket (*No 28*); and the shell and seaweed picture (*No 48*).

Heather Clarke, who designed the home sweet home collage (*No 9*); the Valentine heart (*No 11*); the stencilled cushions (*No 25*); the cat on a mat tapestry (*No 26*); and the handkerchief patchwork bedspread (*No 27*).

Jill Mason, who designed the sleep pillows (*No 35*).

Jane Newdick, who designed the perfumed pomander (*No 2*); the candles (*No 3*); the satin-bound towels (*No 33*); the Christmas crackers (*No 49*); and who made and packaged the preserves (*Nos 12–22*).

Kit Pyman, who designed the macramé stowaway (*No 23*).

Susan Rooke, who designed the woven-on-a-loom tapestry (*No 5*); the quilted bedside rug (*No 7*); the wedding album (*No 8*); the leaf-shaped satin cushions (*No 34*); and the Mondrian-inspired duvet cover (*No 50*).

Celia Rufey, who designed the prettily trimmed pillowcases (*No 1*); and the circular log cabin tablecloth (*No 47*).

Ann Swetman, who designed the Aran bedspread (*No 29*).

Lois Vickers, who designed the embroidered jug of nasturtiums (*No 31*).

Helen Watson, who designed the peg dolls (*No 30*).

Thanks are also due to the following photographers:

Barry Bullough, who photographed *Nos 36–46*.

John Cook, who photographed the cover, and *Nos 3, 6, 8, 12–22, 27, 28, 33, 47, 49* and *50*.

Philip Dowell, who photographed *Nos 2, 26, 32* and *48*.

Melvin Grey, who photographed *No 23*.

Di Lewis, who photographed *Nos 1, 7, 29* and *34*.

Bill McLaughlin, who photographed *No 10*.

Peter Myers, who photographed *No 31*.

Dennis Stone, who photographed *Nos 11, 25* and *30*.